CAN THE EU SPEND BETTER?

About Policy Network

Policy Network is an international thinktank and research institute. Its network spans national borders across Europe and the wider world with the aim of promoting the best progressive thinking on the major social and economic challenges of the 21st century.

Our work is driven by a network of politicians, policymakers, business leaders, public service professionals, and academic researchers who work on long-term issues relating to public policy, political economy, social attitudes, governance and international affairs. This is complemented by the expertise and research excellence of Policy Network's international team.

A platform for research and ideas

- Promoting expert ideas and political analysis on the key economic, social and political challenges of our age.
- Disseminating research excellence and relevant knowledge to a wider public audience through interactive policy networks, including interdisciplinary and scholarly collaboration.
- Engaging and informing the public debate about the future of European and global progressive politics.

A network of leaders, policymakers and thinkers

- Building international policy communities comprising individuals and affiliate institutions.
- Providing meeting platforms where the politically active, and potential leaders of the future, can engage with each other across national borders and with the best thinkers who are sympathetic to their broad aims.
- Engaging in external collaboration with partners including higher education institutions, the private sector, thinktanks, charities, community organisations, and trade unions.
- Delivering an innovative events programme combining in-house seminars with large-scale public conferences designed to influence and contribute to key public debates.

www.policy-network.net

CAN THE EU SPEND BETTER?

An EU Budget for Crises and Sustainability

ROWMAN &
LITTLEFIELD
―――― INTERNATIONAL ――――

London • New York

Published by Rowman & Littlefield International Ltd.
Unit A, Whitacre, 26-34 Stannary Street, London, SE11 4AB
www.rowmaninternational.com

Rowman & Littlefield International Ltd.is an affiliate of Rowman & Littlefield
4501 Forbes Boulevard, Suite 200, Lanham, Maryland 20706, USA
With additional offices in Boulder, New York, Toronto (Canada), and Plymouth (UK)
www.rowman.com

Copyright © 2016 Policy Network

All rights reserved. No part of this book may be reproduced in any form or by
any electronic or mechanical means, including information storage and retrieval
systems, without written permission from the publisher, except by a reviewer who
may quote passages in a review.

British Library Cataloguing in Publication Data
A catalogue record for this book is available from the British Library

ISBN: PB 978-1-78660-284-8
ISBN: eBook 978-1-78660-285-5

Library of Congress Cataloging-in-Publication Data
Library of Congress Control Number: 2016959528

∞™ The paper used in this publication meets the minimum requirements of
American National Standard for Information Sciences—Permanence of Paper
for Printed Library Materials, ANSI/NISO Z39.48-1992.

Printed in the United States of America

CONTENTS

Acknowledgments	vii
Preface	ix
Introduction	1
The EU Budget at a Glance: Key Facts and History	15
Lessons from the 2014–2020 MFF Negotiations	29
The MFF 2014–2020, Two Years On	43
What Can Be Expected from the MFF Mid-Term Review?	59
What Will the EU Budget Look Like after 2020? What Future for the CAP?	75
Conclusion and Recommendations	99
References	105
List of Abbreviations	107

ACKNOWLEDGMENTS

This publication would not have been possible without the financial support of the Royal Society for the Protection of Birds. I would like to thank in particular Stephen Hinchley and Louis Leroy-Warnier for their encouragements and guidance throughout a project which started in early 2016. Despite shared disappointment at the result of the UK's referendum on membership of the EU, I hope that the perspectives shared here will inspire British stakeholders and policymakers in their continuous engagement with the EU.

The publication owes a great debt to Johnny Runge and Florian Ranft who have played a critical role in gathering evidence supporting the report. Thanks also to Ben Dilks for supervising the editing process.

Around 30 individuals from seven different EU countries have been interviewed or consulted between March and August 2016. I would like to express my gratitude to them for taking the time to share their views on sometimes sensitive matters. They include:

- A dozen senior government officials from Germany, France, Poland, the Netherlands and Britain;
- Three members of national parliaments;

- Four advisers to European commissioners or senior European commission officials;
- Six members of the European parliament and their staff;
- Three spokespeople for stakeholder organisations at EU and national level;
- Three academic or policy experts.

Finally, special thanks to two masters of the EU budget and of the common agricultural policy, Alan Matthews and Martin Nesbit, for their very useful feedback on my first draft.

Renaud Thillaye, October 2016

PREFACE

The analysis contained in this book by Renaud Thillaye could not have come at a more appropriate time: indeed, planning for the next mid-term Financial Framework for the EU budget is gradually coming online in Brussels, both within the European commission and the European parliament, and, I am sure, in the majority of the EU member states.

The EU budget represents a mere two per cent of total public spending in the EU and yet it is expected to be a key element for growth, more equal development of its member states, research and innovation and implementation of internal policies, such as agriculture. It also is expected to give the EU a role on the international scene, mainly with regard to developing countries, but rapidly also in the wider foreign and security context.

If the EU has in the past achieved greater cohesion and experienced phases of good growth, it would be mistaken to relate this exclusively to the EU budget. The success has come through a mix of policy design and centrally disbursed funds in line with national, regional and municipal budgets. Coherence has been a major factor, but achieving coherence has been facilitated by common spending priorities.

The present crisis, triggered outside the EU by the collapse of a US bank, Lehman Brothers, has created wide differences in the economic performance of EU member states, and increased inequalities against the trend of the past. Gerhard Schroeder, the former chancellor of Germany, once famously replied to a journalist's question about the more limited German economic growth compared to Portugal, that this was precisely the common objective, to have the weaker economies in Europe catching up, including through EU budget spending, including a large net contribution by Germany. This was a time when solidarity still had a meaning within the European Union.

The crisis has brought more focus on contributions to the budget and return to one's own country. Tight budgets in the majority of member states will make the next period more difficult, as will the decision by the UK to withdraw from the EU. The UK has indeed been a net contributor to the EU's budget.

The last budget planning exercise has already been difficult, as could be expected when a smaller cake has to be split up between more policy priorities. The next planning period is likely to see similar horse trading among policy areas, overshadowed by a growing questioning of common spending altogether. This means that EU spending will have to be orientated towards broad support of citizens, with more transparency on the value added for the Union as a whole, rather than satisfying sectoral interests.

One goal that could unite large parts of the European public is sustainability. The European model, mainly based on social market economy principles, has been attractive even beyond European borders. Europe needs to find economic growth, shared reasonably between its citizens, while respecting the carrying capacity of our planet.

This will require change in present policies, away from fossil-fuel-based energy, towards more dematerialised forms of production and consumption and more consideration for the crucial ecosystems on this planet. The UN has recognised this need in adopting ambitious sustainable development goals.

For the agricultural budget the implications will become rapidly clear: simple sectoral income support, based on acreage, ie helping large farms more than smaller ones, will run into more solid opposition. Agricultural practice which produces collective benefits for employment, decent incomes, the environment and landscape protection may be more palatable to a broader European public and taxpayers.

Renaud argues different scenarios and their likely acceptance among the traditional decision-makers in the commission, parliament and council. I, for one, believe that Europe needs to be bold to regain the support of its citizens: move away from particular sectoral interest towards broad common interests. In my view, the next EU budget should decisively move away from simple agricultural income support in pillar one and shift spending towards rural development objectives based on healthy food produced in decent working conditions, supportive of and using the nature's renewable services.

It may be the only way to maintain a substantial part of the EU budget for agriculture.

Karl Falkenberg was a former director-general for the environment in the EU commission. As special adviser to President Jean-Claude Juncker he has drafted a report on a more sustainable Europe and he is presently a senior fellow at Oxford University. The above text strictly represents the author's personal views and does not, in any way, represent wider institutional views.

INTRODUCTION

The EU budget: What is it for and can it get any better?

"The MFF negotiation is the mother of all EU negotiations." (senior government official)

"This budget looks like nothing. We have no power." (MEP, budgets committee)

KEY POINTS

- The forthcoming EU budget negotiations will be a litmus test for the EU's ability to govern itself and take meaningful, strategic decisions in the current 'existential' crisis.
- The rationale for EU budget reform is strong. However, policymakers and stakeholders should beware of the lure of simplistic ideas such as focusing on the EU's 'own resources', and spending 'more' or 'less' at EU or in specific areas.
- European added value can help reflect on the quality of EU spending, but this concept requires a basic consensus on EU objectives and benchmarks. The Europe 2020 strategy and the EU's post-2020 sustainability strategy, should guide EU 'internal' spending.
- The EU budget offers a wide array of rules and instruments, the impact of which is often underestimated. The focus of negotiations

should, therefore, be as much on *how* EU money is spent as on *how much* and *in which areas*. Reconciling a more conditional and performance-based budget with greater flexibility will be a key challenge for the next MFF.

Amid Brexit, terrorism and the refugee crisis, very few European citizens are aware that the EU is heading towards a new cycle of budgetary discussions. By the end of the year, it will have completed the mid-term review of its 2014–2020 Multiannual Financial Framework (MFF), which sets the parameters for the EU's annual budgets. Next year, it is expected to start discussing the next MFF, which will start after 2020. This schedule is likely to be overshadowed by Britain's exit negotiations from the EU, which are expected to start in 2017. Yet, Brexit will have significant implications for the MFF negotiations by exacerbating tensions between national governments who will have to make up for the UK's net contribution to the EU budget. More significantly, upcoming budget negotiations will be a test for the EU, which will need to demonstrate its capacity to govern itself and make a difference by responding to public preferences in a strategic way.

This report aims to present the key policy and political challenges and opportunities faced by all those who concern themselves with improving the *quality* of EU spending. It starts from the assumption that better and more sustainable economic, social and environmental outcomes along the lines of the Europe 2020 strategy objectives, the Paris climate agreement targets and the UN sustainable development goals can be achieved either by shifting EU expenditure from one area to another, or attaching new strings or rules to it. It argues that focusing on *how* the EU spends rather than *how much* or *in which area* is a politically more tractable approach. The report provides an in-depth focus on environmental and agricultural spending, a major area with a significant impact on sustainability, and in which the gap between what is often deemed desirable and what is politically feasible has long been a concern in many EU countries and across the political spectrum.

The report is divided in six chapters. The following introduction presents the political and conceptual trends which are likely to frame and dominate the budget negotiations in the next few months and years. Chapter 1 provides a brief historical overview on the EU budget key changes from the early 1960s to the MFF 2014–2020. Chapter 2 looks at the main political and policy lessons drawn from the last MFF negotiations. Chapter 3 focuses on what can be learned from two years of implementation. Chapter 4 focuses on the MFF mid-term review which will take place in late 2016 and early 2017. Chapter 5 outlines possible EU budget options after 2020. The conclusions and recommendations suggest ways in which the EU budget can be geared both towards (long-term) sustainability and (short-term, local) flexibility.

I. THE BUDGET TRAP AND THE NEW POLITICS

The EU budget negotiations are possibly one of the most frustrating topic for EU policymakers. Every seven years, EU institutions and member states bicker for months over a few highly symbolic figures, such as the EU's overall spending level (usually around one per cent of the EU's gross national income), individual countries' net balances, rebates and side-payments. Yet what looks like a very epic battle from the outside usually bears only limited results. Like EU institutions, the EU budget is a legacy of past compromises and agreements which are difficult to undo unless the whole equilibrium collapses. To take the most obvious examples, France secured agriculture subsidies early on and still sees them as a pillar of the EU's package. Southern and eastern European countries firmly hang on to cohesion funds, which amount of up to four per cent of their gross national income (GNI) and, in several member states, to more than 50 per cent of public investment (14 per cent in EU average). The UK has long clung on to its rebate negotiated in the early 1980s and a few other member states have obtained 'rebates on the rebate'.

This legacy casts a long shadow over the possibility of changing the main parameters of EU expenditure in a more optimal and strategic direction. On paper, the EU spends its money in three main political fields or what the EU terms 'headings': competitiveness, cohesion and natural resources. In reality, the largest spending item remains direct payments to farmers. They make up for nearly 30 per cent of the EU budget, versus approximatively seven per cent for research and innovation (Horizon 2020) and two per cent for security. In 2011, the European commission tabled a reasonably ambitious proposal for the MFF 2014–2020, with the main objective of aligning the EU budget with the objectives of the Europe 2020 strategy. The intergovernmental negotiations that followed reduced the scope for change, in particular on competitiveness, security and external action.

EU budgetary questions are highly salient and politicised in national contexts as they provide a rare tangible (though narrow and biased) picture of how each individual country benefits from the EU. Although regularly denounced by pro-Europeans and the European commission, the 'net balance' approach usually dwarfs any attempt to think in terms of collective and long-term European interests. From Margaret Thatcher's famous "I want my money back" to the Leave campaign's unfounded claim that Brexit would bring £350m a week back to London, Britain has played a leading role in demonising EU spending. During the most recent MFF negotiations, David Cameron very firmly – and successfully – advocated a real term cut in the EU budget for the first time.

Yet, the anti-EU mood is not confined to the UK. Trust in the EU has sharply deteriorated since the global financial crisis. There are perceptions that the EU spends on remote and dubious things while national and local governments have to tighten their belt. The backlash is particularly pronounced in western and northern Europe (see figure i.1), where most countries are net contributors and where populist parties regularly attack the EU's waste of money and the very principle of a common pot.

If the politics is not favourable to more EU spending, the rationale for spending radically less is not obvious either. In the last few

INTRODUCTION

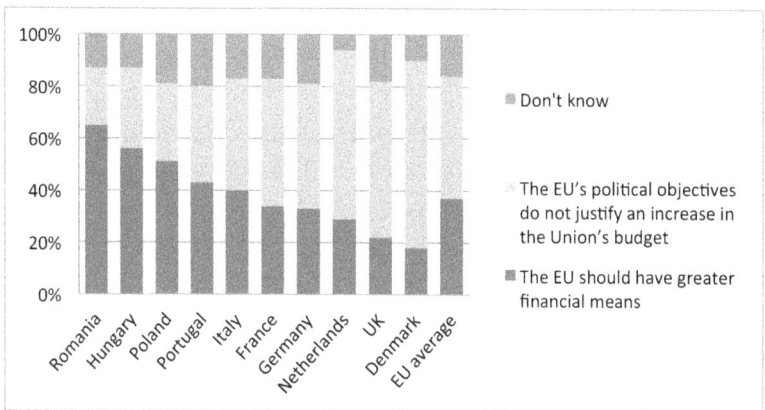

Figure i.1 Public attitudes towards the overall level of EU spending in selected member states (2015).

years, EU officials and MEPs have increasingly complained about under-budgeting and an EU budget 'not fit for purpose'. From their perspective national governments need to match the very high objectives they assign to the EU with the requisite financial resources. The completion of the last MFF (2007–2013) was marked by a serious 'backlog' in payments which is likely to re-occur at the end of the current framework unless 'commitments' are backed by the same level of payments.

Governments find it hard to admit that EU spending has, in fact, become a necessity more than a luxury if the EU is to become more operational and effective. First, deteriorating social and fiscal situations in southern Europe mean that the EU provides much-needed investments and social programmes. Stopping these transfers would cause havoc. Second, the refugee crisis and new security threats demand greater joint efforts towards the management of external borders and the absorption of the nearly 2 million migrants who filed an application for asylum in the EU over the course of 2014 and 2015. Third, the EU needs to engineer an industrial transition towards low-carbon, high value-added production which necessitates large and coordinated upfront investments. Finally, calls for a euro area budget capacity have become more vocal in the hope that such an instrument would help address cyclical and/or structural imbalances.

In short, the EU budget is severely stretched between contradictory forces: politics on the one hand, and economic and geopolitical challenges on the other. It finds itself at the core of a long-standing EU dilemma, namely the tension between the logics of integration and the obstinate centrality of national politics. A key question for the near future is therefore what routes and arguments are available to those who wish to reform it. How can the budget trap be avoided and can we make more of the existing level of resources while reconciling diverging expectations? Can the EU budget be made both more flexible and more transformative? Can concerns over net contributions and cross-EU redistribution be alleviated by producing higher value for money?

2. OWN RESOURCES, WRONG ANSWER?

There is no silver bullet to the budget trap. Yet, shifting the public attention away from the expenditure side of things is often seen as one of them. In December 2013, at the end of painful and protracted MFF negotiations, the three main EU institutions established a "High level working group on own resources" chaired by former commissioner and Italian prime minister Mario Monti. The group is expected to deliver recommendations in December 2016. Its mission is to recommend ways in which the EU could more directly access its own 'genuine' resources rather than rely, for more than 80 per cent of its budget, on GNI-based national contributions.

The rationale behind appointing the group may be strong. Its intermediary diagnosis of a complex, unstable and ultimately distorting resources system bears a lot of plausibility.[1] However, its objective to "return to financing mechanisms that are closer to the original intention of the treaties so that discussions on the EU budget in the future could focus more on the actual content of EU policies rather than being almost exclusively devoted to the calculation of net budgetary positions" (p.19) sounds far-fetched. Equipping the EU with direct tax revenues equates to shifting resources away from national control to the EU level, something which is unlikely to fly in the current context. Past attempts to harmonise national tax bases have proved difficult, not least the recent proposal for a harmonised corporate tax base. Governments would be likely to keep a close eye on the level of taxes raised in their country and use it as a leverage tool in budget negotiations. Finally, and perhaps most importantly, such a move would not remove the widespread suspicion that the EU does not spend well and on the right things. Much more needs to be done to raise the level of trust in EU spending.

3. THE OVERLOOKED POWER OF THE EU BUDGET

A good place to start from is to consider the power and potential of the budget in its current form. At a first glance, one per cent of the EU's GNI (and approximatively two per cent of EU public spending) offers only limited capacity for action. There are nonetheless several ways in which the EU manages to punch above its weight.

First, administrative spending (staff and running costs) is limited to approximately six per cent of the EU budget, while the rest of expenditure goes either directly to EU citizens (notably farmers and students) or provides project-based support to public authorities and businesses. By comparison, the French state spends about 30 per cent on payroll. The EU is not a state and it does not provide frontline public services.

Second, European structural and investment funds (ESI funds), which represent almost half of the EU budget, are conditioned on national co-financing (rates vary from 50 to 100 per cent depending on regional levels of development and country-specific situations). This means that EU spending very often triggers a 'top-up' at national or regional level and, therefore, has a decisive impact on the structure of national spending. Over 2014–2020, ESI funds are expected to represent 14 per cent of public investment, a figure well above 30 per cent in a dozen of countries.[2] This coordination function of the EU budget is often overlooked.

Third, in addition to grants and subsidies, the EU has recently developed 'financial instruments' such as loans, guarantees and equity, which have higher leverage. Alongside the Competitiveness of Enterprises and Small and Medium-sized Enterprises programme (COSME), the launch of the Investment Plan for Europe (2015–2018) epitomises this trend, which consists in attracting private investors into funds alimented and guaranteed by the EU. Financial instruments give risky projects a chance and mobilise private capital in the same way as ESI funds mobilise (mainly) public investment.

Finally, important strings are attached to EU spending. Over the past 20 years, ex-ante impact assessment, ex-post evaluation and conditionality have expanded in a spectacular way, thus improving the quality of spending and ensuring the delivery of specific public goods. It takes several forms: horizontal rules of programming, reporting, monitoring, evaluation to be put in place by recipients of EU grants; 'ex-ante' and 'macroeconomic' conditionalities attached to ESI funds to make sure the conditions for impactful expenditure are in place; six per cent performance reserve to be released at the end of the MFF (ESI funds); health and safety 'cross-compliance' rules and 'greening' requirements attached to agricultural subsidies; Failing to observe common rules can lead the EU to withhold or suspend funds.

Financial leverage and conditionality are therefore the main ways in which the EU budget makes most of its limited volume. Tapping this overlooked power to raise the quality of EU spending could go a long way to addressing public mistrust. Nevertheless, this requires clarity as to what is meant by 'quality spending'. Beyond natural political disagreements on how much, what and how the EU should spend, EU experts and institutions have long tried to offer concepts and theories to the public in an attempt to rationalise EU budget reforms. The last section of this introduction presents an overview of the theoretical tools available from expert or institutional literature.

4. ASSESSING THE QUALITY OF THE EU BUDGET

Assessing the quality of the EU budget opens three main types of questions. First, should parts of the EU budget be moved down to national budgets and vice-versa? Second, does the EU budget target the right objectives at the right of expenditure? Third, does the EU budget use the right channels and tools to allocate resources? As this report argues, stakeholders and policy-makers should dedicate greater attention to the third question.

Why spend at EU level?

Looking at government theory is a first way to approach the EU budget debate. According to the classification developed by Richard Musgrave (1959), government spending splits into three broad categories: allocation of resources, income redistribution and macroeconomic stabilisation. The EU budget is mainly about the first function, with only limited involvement in stabilisation in the euro area and income redistribution (arguably, direct payments to farmers and grants to less developed regions have both a redistribution and allocation function). Government intervention in the form of allocation is usually justified by four types of market failures: the provision of public goods (for instance, clean air and water); externalities (such as unintended consequences of individual action); asymmetric information; and economies of scale (for instance, natural monopolies). The wide range of EU budgetary interventions ticks all these boxes, from the economies of scale expected from 'giant' projects such as Cern (the European Organization for Nuclear Research, based in Geneva), Galileo (Europe's Global Satellite Navigation System), and Iter (the international nuclear fusion reactor currently being built in southern France) to 'climate mainstreaming' providing for 20 per cent of climate-relate expenditure throughout the budget.

Fiscal federalism takes this reasoning a step further by looking at the most optimal level of intervention. Roughly speaking, centralisation is justified if economies of scale can be obtained and negative externalities internalised at a higher level. Decentralisation is desirable when significant differences in needs and in preferences have to be taken into account. As Alesina et al (2005, p.276) put it in the wake of the EU's eastern enlargement, this implies a "trade-off between the benefits of centralisation, arising from economies of scale or externalities, and the costs of harmonising policies in the light of the increased heterogeneity of individual preferences in a union which is growing in size."

Ecorys et al (2008) developed a comprehensive "subsidiarity test" of the EU budget based on fiscal federalism and political economy arguments. They found that a substantial part of cohesion and agricultural spending should return to the national level, while there should be greater EU spending (either by moving national programmes up to the EU level or spending more on existing EU programmes) on research, defence, foreign aid, cross-border networks and the environment. These findings converge with most recent normative studies on the EU budget, although most of them admit that political and institutional inertia – and the presence of numerous veto players – explain the current structure of the EU budget.

Spend on what? European added value and the Europe 2020 strategy

The concept of "European added value" (EAV) has been central to MFF negotiations for a decade and it is likely to remain a key benchmark used by proponents of EU budget reform. However, there is no single definition of EAV, something which underlines the blurry nature of the concept. In the context of EU budget discussions, policymakers and stakeholders often use EAV as a proxy for European collective interest by opposition to national net returns. In a 2014 review on financial management risks,[3] the European court of auditors wrote:

> "The commission, with the support of the European parliament and the council, should prioritise spending on activities where there is European added value, such as areas where the commission has sole

competence, cross-border actions, projects promoting common interest and European networks. Budget areas characterised by the multiplicity and fragmentation of spending, or where commitments and national allocations are slowly utilised, or underused, all merit extra scrutiny, with a possible view to cancelling the funding."

Such a vision implies fundamentally restructuring the EU budget, especially by reducing EU co-funding of regional or national projects. Not only is this hardly feasible in the short term, but it misses the potential to steer and improve local practices through EU funding. Indeed, there is no such thing as the provision of 'genuine' European public goods in opposition to national or local public goods since local projects co-funded by the EU often pursue both.

A more elaborate definition of EAV is the EU's ability to wield higher net returns than the same level of aggregate national spending (Bertelsmann Stiftung, 2013). In a report on the commission's MFF proposal,[4] the House of Lords EU committee concluded: "EAV is a subjective and, in the end, political quantity; but this does not make it meaningless. It is the obverse of subsidiarity; where it is present, EU spending definitely achieves more than spending by member states."

In the absence of an uncontested benchmark of EAV, decision-makers need to define more clearly, and perhaps quantify, what the objectives of EU spending are. They could, on the one hand, use more explicitly the EU's long-term political goals enshrined in the Europe 2020 strategy. The five headline targets on employment, R&D, climate-energy, education and poverty provide a strong compass, at least for EU 'internal spending' (headings one and two of the MFF). The European commission called its 2011 MFF proposal "A budget for Europe 2020," reflecting the fact that most proposed changes aimed to align the budget more closely with the Europe 2020 goals.[5] This approach is justified in terms of EAV by the fact that member states' structural divergences would ultimately create negative externalities and prevent them from achieving desired European public goods. In its report on the EU's 2014 annual accounts, the court of auditors wrote: "member states give inadequate attention to Europe

2020 achievements in partnership agreements and programmes. Both issues limit the commission's ability to monitor and report on performance and the contribution of the EU budget to Europe 2020." In the wake of the UN sustainable development goals adopted in 2015, the forthcoming revised EU strategy for sustainability should also serve as a compass for future EU budgets.[6]

On the other hand, EAV has to do with common external challenges and threats. The rationale for pooling resources at EU level is high when it comes to tackling illegal immigration, cross-border trafficking and internal and external security threats. With less than 10 per cent of the EU budget dedicated to these objectives, the margin of progress is significant.

How to spend? Instruments, rules and flexibility

As suggested above, the EU budget has more power than it is usually assumed. This is due to the leverage capacity of ESI funds and financial instruments, as well as to the rules attached to EU spending. While the political scope for shuffling around large blocks of EU spending will probably remain limited in the next few years, changes in the EU's intervention channels and conditions offer a silver lining. Several options will be available to EU policymakers in the next few years, such as transforming a greater share of EU funds into financial instruments, strengthening horizontal rules (for instance, by extending them to aspects of the rule of law and democracy), extending environmental conditionality, etc.

Nevertheless, rules and conditionalities are also criticised for their bureaucratic character. Attaching more strings to EU programmes risks making the budget more rigid, complex and less accessible. Its reactivity to new events might be diminished. As the controversy around the 'greening' of farm subsidies shows, reinforcing them runs the risk of a backlash which could lead to throwing the baby out with the bathwater and drop higher environmental ambitions outright. For these reasons, the flexibility of the EU budget is likely to dominate future debates. Several flexibility instruments were introduced into the EU budget during the last MFF negotiations, but they have already been largely used up.

Like EAV, flexibility is an ill-defined concept often used by politicians and policymakers to say different things: the possibility of shifting money across the main budget headings; reserving a larger share of the budget for unforeseen events and circumstances; giving national governments and regions the choice of taking part in specific programmes of not, and the possibility of choosing from a menu of implementing options; and leaving more room for national state aid. All these options are likely to be on the table of the MFF mid-term review and of the next MFF negotiations. As this report argues, reconciling flexibility with higher ambitions may necessitate developing the contractual dimension of EU spending. This requires setting uncontested EU objectives and benchmarks on the one hand, and giving more space for a bottom-up, context-based identification of the means to achieve these outcomes.

NOTES

1. "High Level Group on Own Resources. First assessment report. Brussels, 17 December 2015." Accessed August 2016. http://ec.europa.eu/budget/library/biblio/documents/multiannual_framework/HLGOR_1stassessment2014final_en.pdf

2. "Investing in jobs and growth - maximising the contribution of European Structural and Investment Funds." European commission communication, December 14, 2015, COM(2015) 639 final. Accessed August 2016. http://ec.europa.eu/contracts_grants/pdf/esif/invest-progr-investing-job-growth-report_en.pdf p.4

3. "Making the best use of EU money: a landscape review of the risks to the financial management of the EU budget." Last modified on November 25, 2014. http://www.eca.europa.eu/en/Pages/NewsItem.aspx?nid=5361

4. "European Union Committee - Thirteenth Report EU Financial Framework from 2014." Last modified on March 22, 2011. http://www.publications.parliament.uk/pa/ld201011/ldselect/ldeucom/125/12505.htm#note14

5. "A Budget for Europe 2020." European commission communication, June 29, 2011, COM(2011) 500 final. Accessed August 2016. http://ec.europa.eu/health/programme/docs/maff-2020_en.pdf

6. In its work programme for 2016, the European commission announced an initiative towards a "new approach to ensuring Europe's economic growth and social and environmental sustainability beyond the 2020 timeframe." See "Commission Work Programme 2016: No time for business as usual." European commission communication, October 27, 2015, COM(2015) 610 final, http://ec.europa.eu/atwork/pdf/cwp_2016_en.pdf, 5

THE EU BUDGET AT A GLANCE
Key facts and history

KEY POINTS

- The MFF sets the main parameters of the EU's annual budgeting process. While 80 per cent of the EU's financial resources come directly from member states' contributions, the European council plays a major role in the decision-making. The European parliament can use its veto power to obtain a maximum of concessions.
- The EU budget's structure has significantly changed over time, with the rise of the cohesion policy, research and innovation, external action and security. From 75 per cent in the early 1970s, the share of agriculture has come down to 38 per cent.
- Compared with the MFF 2007–2013, the MFF 2014–2020 is characterised by a sharp increase in competitiveness and security spending, albeit still modest in numerical terms, and a decline in cohesion and natural resources expenditure. Flexibility instruments still represent less than one per cent of the EU budget.
- The CAP has gone through substantial change since its inception, especially by removing harmful production subsidies. Nevertheless, direct income support to farmers still represent 74 per cent of EU spending towards 'natural resources'.

1. THE EU BUDGET: THE BASICS

The MFF and annual budgets

Like any public or private organisation, the EU has an annual budget, which is debated every year by the European parliament. However, key negotiations take place every seven years, when the EU's Multiannual Financial Framework (MFF) is decided upon. The MFF lays down the maximum annual amounts ('ceilings') which the EU may spend in different political fields ('headings'). The MFF is therefore not the budget itself, but the basis for the annual budgeting process.[1]

The MFF's objective is to ensure predictability, to keep expenditure in line with political priorities and to respect the limits of the EU's own resources. It also aims to avoid difficult budgetary negotiations between member states every year. The MFF was introduced in 1988 after recurring budgetary crises in 1970s and 1980s, involving standoffs between the European parliament and the council, which led to the failure to adopt a budget in 1980, 1985, 1986, and 1988 until the financial year was well underway. In 2009, the Lisbon treaty formalised the MFF, which today requires a council regulation covering a period of at least five years (Article 312 of the Treaty on the Functioning of the European Union, TFEU). The current MFF was agreed in 2013 and runs between 2014 and 2020. It allows the EU to spend €960bn in commitments (one per cent of GNI) and €908bn in payments (in 2011 prices).

Expenditure: commitments and payments

On the expenditure side, the MFF distinguishes between 'commitment appropriations' and 'payment appropriations':

- Commitments cover the costs of legal obligations, such as contracts or grants, which the EU may sign in a financial year of the MFF. They are the amounts the EU promises in a given year but which may be spent in that same year or over several years.

- Payments cover expenditure actually spent in a given year of the MFF. This is expenditure arising from commitments made in the same year or in previous years.

Revenues: state-based 'own' resources

EU expenditure is determined by a revenue ceiling, and not the other way round. The EU cannot borrow to finance its deficit or some specific activities. As part of the MFF legislative package, the 'own resources decision', which is adopted unanimously by all member states and ratified by national parliaments, sets a ceiling for revenues. The decision for 2014–2020 caps the total amount of own resources to 1.23 per cent of the EU's GNI. In practice, in the recent and current MFF, ceilings for commitments and payments have been set well below own resources ceiling, typically around one per cent.[2]

The EU's 'own resources' combine three main types of revenue:

- Traditional own resources (TOR): They consist mainly of customs duties on imports from outside the EU and of sugar levies.
- VAT-based resources: A uniform rate of 0.3 per cent of the harmonised VAT base is transferred to the EU budget from each member state.
- GNI-based contributions: A standard percentage is levied on member states' GNIs. Although this is a 'top-up', and is sometimes referred to as 'additional' or 'residual' own resources, it funds the part of the budget which is not covered by other sources of income and represents around 75 per cent of overall own resources (see figure 1.1).

With TOR making up only 10 per cent of the EU budget, it is clear that 'own resources' remain firmly in the hands of member states. What was meant to be a transitory principle (tax-based resources shuffled through member states) has become the rule. As Ciprianni (2014, p.10) puts it, "member states have remained in the end the (pay)masters. Under the current circumstances, EU 'financial

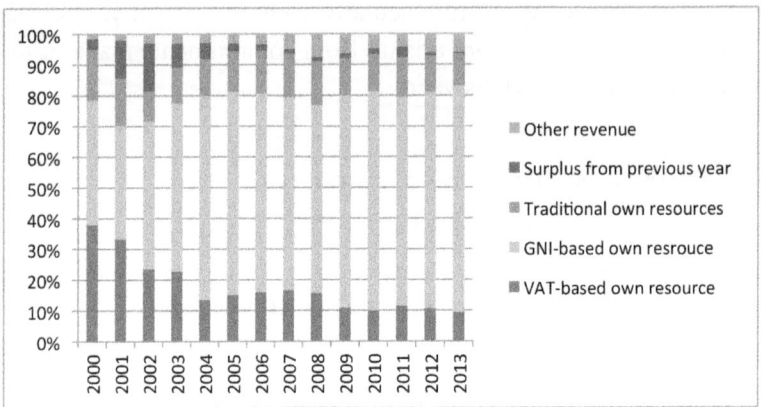

Figure 1.1 The EU's own resources over time (2000–2013). *Source*: Own adaptation from European commission, EU budget 2013 financial report (Annex 2.b).

autonomy' means no more than member states complying with the obligation they have set on themselves to finance each year the EU budget within the limits of the MFF-agreed ceiling."

Rebates for large net contributors

The balance between expenditure and resources leaves member states either net contributors to, or net beneficiaries from, the EU budget. Some of the largest imbalances have been corrected over time. As part of the Fontainebleau deal in 1984, the UK government obtained a 66 per cent rebate on its net contribution to the Common Agricultural Policy (CAP) and cohesion funds. However, after the post-2004 enlargements, the decision to exclude non-agricultural spending towards new member states from the calculation reduced the rebate's significance.[3] Also, net contributors such as Germany, the Netherlands, Austria and Sweden have secured a cap on their contributions to the British rebate since 2001, a reduced call rate on VAT and a reduction in their annual GNI contribution since 2007. The Netherlands also obtained an increase in the retained share of collection costs of traditional own resources from 10 per cent over

1970–2000 to 25 per cent since 2001, something which now applies to all member states (20 per cent under the current MFF).

Decision-making and key players

The MFF decision-making is a special legislative procedure combining intergovernmental and supranational elements. The MFF is a regulation proposed by the commission and unanimously agreed in the council, which requires the consent of the European parliament by absolute majority voting (TFEU Article 312). This does not allow the parliament to introduce amendments to the regulation, but gives MEPs a veto: pending their approval, the conclusions of the negotiations in the council are nothing more than a political agreement.

In practice, however, the European council plays a very important role. As Matthews (2014, p.183) puts it: "It has become the norm that the actual decision on the MFF ceilings is taken by the European council and later confirmed by the general affairs council." This is justified by the strategic guidance role which EU treaties confer upon the European council, and by the fact that national governments carefully watch the impact of the agreed ceilings and headings figures on their net payment position. This explains the very prominent role played by European council president Herman Van Rompuy in the months leading up to the February 2013 agreement. One implication is that the European council's budgetary discussions spill over into legislative discussions, for instance on the nature of agricultural spending (see section 1.4 below).

The negotiations of the MFF 2014–2020 saw a very active and determined parliament using every formal and informal opportunity to exercise its powers to the full. For instance, the parliament did not wait for the commission's proposal before adopting its own resolution on the MFF in 2011. MEPs also drafted position papers on contentious issues during the negotiations in the Council. They met the council's 'trio presidency' – the three member states which will hold the presidency over a given 18-month period – ahead of council meetings, and, at the end of the process, used their veto power to negotiate concessions.

Annual budgets

The procedure is slightly different for the annual budget, leaving more space for the European parliament to make amendments. By 1 September of each year, the European commission must table the proposal for the draft budget of the following financial year based on the overall ceilings laid out in the MFF.[4] By 1 October, the council must adopt its position on the draft budget and communicate it to the European parliament. Following the council's communication, the European parliament has 42 days either to approve or to amend the council's position. If the two institutions adopt, and maintain, different positions, a conciliation committee composed of an equal number of representatives of the council and the parliament is convened and has 21 days to agree on a joint text, with the commission acting as an 'honest broker'.[5]

2. THE 2014–2020 MFF IN THE PERSPECTIVE OF THE EU BUDGET HISTORY

The EU budget over time

The first MFF ran for five years (1988–1992), while subsequent ones have each covered seven years (1993–1999, 2000–2006 and 2007–2013). It is nevertheless possible to track the structure of the EU budget back to the early years of the European Economic Community (see table 1.2). Agriculture represented 75 per cent of EU spending in 1972, before the UK joined the EEC. It then fell progressively to 45 per cent by 2006, while structural funds rose sharply from four to 30 per cent. The creation of the European regional development fund (ERDF) in 1972 and of the cohesion fund in 1994 added to the already existing European social fund (ESF) and the

Table 1.2 The EU budget structure over time (1972–2006)

		1972	1980	1987	1994	2001	2006
Agriculture (EAGGF 'guarantee' section)		**75**	**69**	**63.3**	**53.6**	**51.1**	**45.9**
Structural funds		**4.1**	**11**	**16.2**	**25.8**	**27.4**	**30**
	Rural development	1.6	1.9	2.2	4	1.6	3
	ERDF, ESF and cohesion funds	2.5	9.1	14	21.7	17.8	24.5
	Research	2.3	2.2	2.7	4	3.8	4.6
External action		**2.2**	**3.7**	**2.2**	**5**	**5.1**	**4.6**
Administration		**5.3**	**5**	**4.7**	**5.8**	**5.9**	**6**
EU development fund		4	2.9	2.3	2.9	1.9	2.6

Source: Own adaptation from the European commission, EU budget Financial Report 2008.

'guidance' pillar of the European agricultural guidance and guarantee fund (the future European agricultural fund for rural development, EAFRD). The European maritime and fisheries fund (EMFF) and the environmental programme LIFE were also launched in the early 1990s.

The 2007–2014 MFF introduced a new structure, with five headings and a few 'special instruments' outside of the EU budget (table 1.3):

On its website, the European commission claims that each of its financial frameworks has reflected the political priorities of the day. For instance, the first financial framework (1988–1992) initiated by Jacques Delors marked an increase in research and development spending to accompany the completion of the single market. The second framework (1993–1999) was characterised by an increase in social spending, with the view of boosting convergence before the introduction of the euro. The Agenda 2000 (2000–2006) focused on enlargement. Finally, the MFF 2007–2013 gave priority to sustainable growth and competitiveness.[6] In reality, although shifts in expenditure have been real, agriculture still represents 38 per cent of the EU budget today (see graph 1.4).

Table 1.3 Structure of the EU budget from 2007 onwards

MFF heading	Sub-headings and policies	Before 2007
Heading 1: Smart and inclusive growth	*1.a: competitiveness for growth and jobs* Research and innovation; education and training; trans-European networks in energy, transport and telecommunications; development of enterprises, etc.	Research
	1.b: Economic, social and territorial cohesion Cohesion policy	ESF, ERDF, Cohesion fund
Heading 2: Sustainable growth: natural resources	European Agricultural Guarantee Fund (CAP 'pillar 1')	EAGGF guarantee section
	European Agricultural Fund for Rural Development (EARDF, CAP 'pillar 2'), EMF (fisheries fund), LIFE (environment)	EAGGF guidance section
Heading 3: Security and citizenship	Justice and home affairs, border protection, immigration and asylum policy, public health, consumer protection, culture, youth, information and dialogue with citizens.	
Heading 4: Global Europe	External action ('foreign policy') by the EU such as development assistance or humanitarian aid with the exception of the European Development Fund (EDF)	
Heading 5: Administration	administrative expenditure of all the European institutions, pensions and European Schools	
Special instruments and flexibility mechanisms	Emergency Aid Reserve, European Globalisation Fund, Solidarity Fund, Flexibility Instrument, Contingency margin (since 2014)	
Outside the EU budget	European Development Fund (direct contributions from EU Member States)	

Source: Own adaption from European commission.

Highlights from the 2014–2020 MFF

The 2014–2020 MFF does not differ radically from the 2007–2013 MFF. It has five main characteristics. First, an overall real terms reduction in commitments and payments by 3.5 and 3.7 per cent respectively, a first in the history of the EU budget.[7]

THE EU BUDGET AT A GLANCE

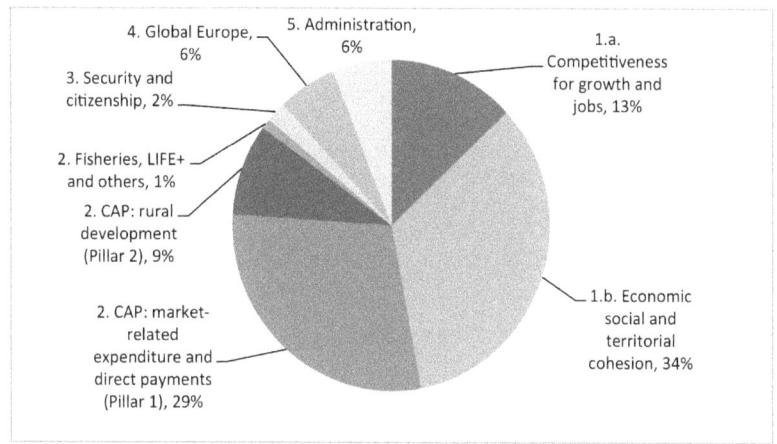

Figure 1.4 Composition of the MFF 2014–2020 (headings and sub-headings). *Source*: European commission.

Second, research and investment expenditure increased by 37.3 per cent compared to 2007–2013. However, in volume, this represents a modest increase relatively to cohesion and agricultural spending. Also, the commission's proposal was much more ambitious than the final outcome (see section 2).

Third, cohesion and 'natural resources' spending decreased in similar proportions, by eight and 11 per cent respectively. Heading two not only contracted from 42 per cent in the MFF 2007–2013 to 39 per cent, but also saw a significant reduction of financial resources in real terms. In particular, CAP pillar one (direct payments to farmers) saw its share decline from 32.1 to 28.9 per cent, with a decrease of 12.9 per cent in real terms.

Fourth, the EU budget remains characterised by the domination of internal and economic items over security and external affairs. Money for 'justice and home affairs' (heading three), which includes border management, immigration and police cooperation, increased by 27 per cent. Still, in absolute terms, this item represents only two per cent of total EU spending. At six per cent, external action and administration remain in line with past MFF.

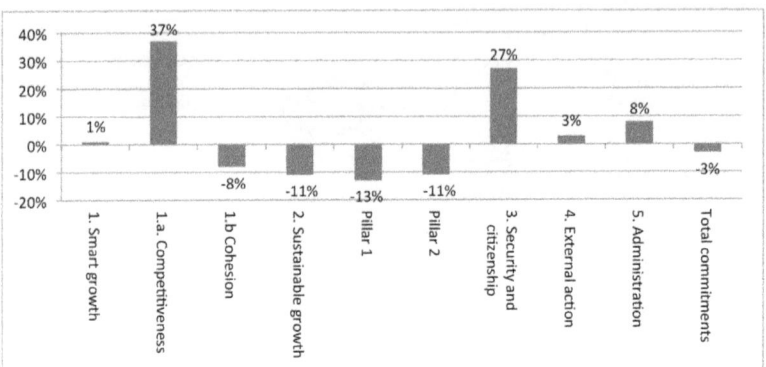

Figure 1.5 MFF headings 2014–2020 compared with 2007–2013 (commitments). *Source*: European commission.

Finally, the MFF 2014–2020 is characterised by the expansion of 'special instruments' which stand outside the MFF and provide extra flexibility, although they still represent less than one per cent of the EU budget. Resources outside the MFF include two types of instruments:[8]

- Instruments providing additional commitments and payments, such as the emergency aid reserve (humanitarian, civilian crisis management and protection operations in non-EU countries), the European globalisation adjustment fund (EGAF, support to workers made redundant as a result of major structural changes in world trade patterns), and the solidarity fund (emergency financial aid following a major disaster in a member state or candidate country). The EGAF and the solidarity fund used to be part of the MFF. They may have been placed outside the MFF in an attempt to make the reduction in MFF headings more visible. Both were substantially reduced, by 70 per cent and 50 per cent respectively (Anania and Pupo d'Andrea, 2015, p.41–42).
- Instruments offering flexibility in comparison with ceilings, in particular the flexibility instrument (funding for "clearly identified expenses" which cannot be covered by the EU budget without exceeding the available ceilings) and the new contingency margin

(last-resort instrument in unforeseen circumstances. Its use must be offset by a corresponding reduction in the MFF ceilings).

3. THE CAP AND NATURAL RESOURCES SPENDING: THE CHANGES FROM WITHIN

The common agricultural policy today has little in common with how it looked 40 years ago. Not only has agricultural spending declined over time, but its very nature has changed. As figure 1.6 shows, 'market interventions', ie price support, were until the 1990s the main instrument. After the 1992 MacSharry reform, support to prices was set at a much lower level, thus discouraging production in an attempt to put an end to surpluses and market distortions. Over 20 years, a system of 'decoupled direct payments' was put in place whereby farmers receive subsidies independently from their level of production and based on the used land surface. Progressivity, environmental conditionality and rural development gained in

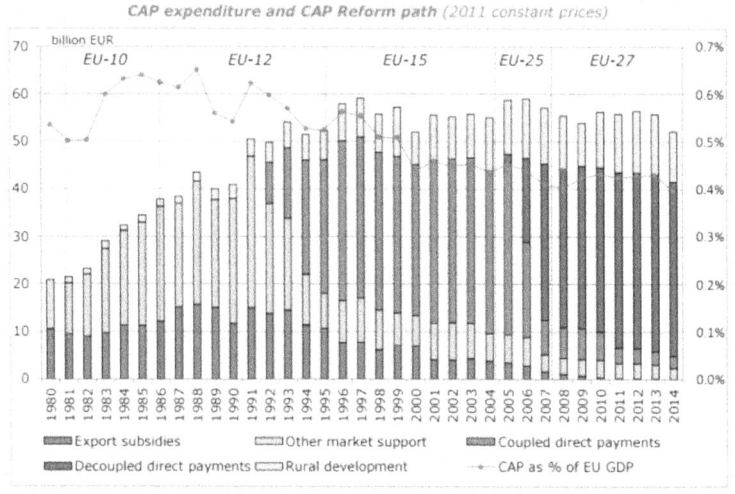

Figure 1.6 CAP expenditure and CAP reform path (2011 constant prices).
Source: European commission.

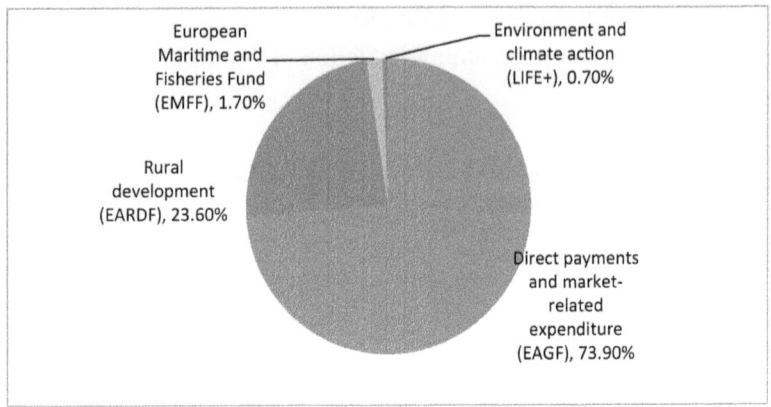

Figure 1.7 **Main components of natural resources spending (heading two), MFF 2014–2020.** *Source*: European commission.

importance. Above all, the CAP has become more decentralised and flexible, with a lot of discretion left to national and regional implementing authorities.

As figure 1.7 illustrates, under the 2014–2020 MFF, 74 per cent of heading two ('natural resources') is in the form of direct payments to farmers (EAGF), which represent 29 per cent of the EU budget. The rural development fund makes up for much of the remaining 26 per cent. Like other structural funds, it is co-managed and co-financed by member states and regions. This leaves only a few millions to the maritime and fisheries fund (EMFF) and to the LIFE+ programme, an environmental fund directly managed by the EU. Such a structure raises questions as to the capacity of the EU to produce environmental public goods.

NOTES

1. "The Multiannual Financial Framework explained." Accessed August 2016. http://ec.europa.eu/budget/mff/introduction/index_en.cfm.

2. "High Level Group on Own Resources. First assessment report. Brussels, 17 December 2015." Accessed August 2016 http://ec.europa.eu/budget/

library/biblio/documents/multiannual_framework/HLGOR_1stassessment 2014final_en.pdf

3. "The UK 'rebate' on the EU budget. An explanation of the abatement and other correction mechanisms." European parliament briefing, February 2016, accessed August 2016, http://www.europarl.europa.eu/RegData/etudes/BRIE/2016/577973/EPRS_BRI(2016)577973_EN.pdf

4. In practice, the proposal is usually presented by June at the latest. For instance, the 2017 budget proposal was presented by the commission on June 30, 2016.

5. If the conciliation committee fails to find an agreement, the commission must submit a new draft budget, on which negotiations between the parliament and the council can restart. If there is no agreement and final adoption of the budget by 31 December, the system of 'provisional twelfths' kicks in (Article 315 TFEU): this means that the maximum amount that the EU is allowed to spend monthly for each category of expenditure equals one twelfth of the relevant appropriations in the previous year's budget or in the draft budget (whichever is the lower).

6. "Multiannual Financial Framework (MFF): Questions and answers." Accessed August 2016. http://europa.eu/rapid/press-release_MEMO-11-468_en.htm

7. If taking into account the change in the composition of the EU, ie excluding Croatia, then reduction for EU-27 is 4.8 per cent (Aniana and Pupo d'Andrea, p.40)

8. Source: European commission, ibid.

LESSONS FROM THE 2014–2020 MFF NEGOTIATIONS

KEY POINTS

- The completion of the 2014–2020 MFF negotiations took more than three years.
- National governments had the upper hand on the overall amount of spending and headings ceilings, triggering the first real-term budget cut in EU history.
- The European commission had some success at streamlining the budget towards the Europe 2020 priorities and the European parliament can be credited for pushing the logic of flexibility and highlighting the risk of payments crises in the face of spending cuts.
- As occurred seven years earlier, member states' net returns and the respective benefits they draw from cohesion policy and the CAP led to three informal coalitions: 'friends of better spending', 'friends of cohesion' and 'friends of agriculture'. The strength of net contributors' preferences, the agreement between Germany and France on protecting the CAP, and divisions between cohesion countries explain the final outcome.

I. HOW THE NEGOTIATION UNFOLDED

It took three years to reach a final agreement on the MFF 2014–2020. Its main outcomes were an overall real-term reduction in EU spending, based on a significant reduction in cohesion and agriculture expenditure, and greater flexibility. The main steps of the negotiation phase are described below:

- June 2010: The European parliament establishes the special committee on policy challenges and budgetary resources for a sustainable European Union after 2013 (SURE).
- June 2011: Adoption of the SURE committee report on "Investing in the future: a new MFF for a competitive, sustainable and inclusive Europe."
- June 2011: Commission's proposal for the MFF 2014–2020 + 60 legislative proposals covering all multi-annual spending programmes.
- May 2012: Council's first negotiating box, which introduced the main elements and options of the negotiation.
- October 2012: New parliament resolution "in the interests of achieving a positive outcome of the MFF 2014–2020 approval procedure."
- November 2012: No agreement reached at a special meeting of the European council.
- February 2013: Agreement reached in the European council.
- March 2013: Parliament resolution on European council conclusions.
- May 2013: First official 'trilogue' meeting between parliament, council and commission.
- June 2013: Tripartite agreement on the MFF.
- November 2013: Parliament gives formal consent to the MFF.
- December 2013: Formal adoption of the MFF legislative package by the council.

The European parliament's position and role

Though holding no formal role other than a power of consent, the European parliament made its position known through various legislative and non-legislative steps throughout the negotiation process, and was consulted by the presidencies before and after council discussions on the MFF. Regular meetings between the presidents of the three main institutions took place (under the provision set by Article 324 TFEU), to which the president of the European council was often invited.

Before the commission formally launched negotiations, the parliament tabled a very ambitious opinion on the desired shape of MFF. The 2011 SURE committee report proposed the following:

- Increase in the size of the MFF by five per cent to reach 1.11 per cent of the EU GNI;
- More flexibility: unspent funds or margins should be transferred from one year to the next, and between spending categories;
- Compulsory mid-term revision clause;
- Reform of own resources;
- A budget cycle of five years, in line with appointments and elections to the EU institutions, increasing political and democratic responsibility, legitimacy and accountability.

This ambitious opinion was endorsed by an overwhelming centre-right and centre-left majority, including the Greens but without the support of the Conservative group (ECR) (figure 2.1).

In 2012, the European parliament reiterated its main positions and reacted to the commission's proposal of a freeze of the MFF 2014–2020 ceilings at 2013 levels. The resolution pointed out that this would "not be sufficient to finance existing policy priorities

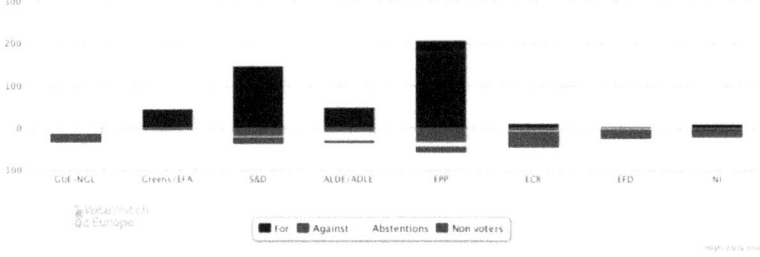

Figure 2.1   European parliament resolution for a new MFF (2011) – Vote breakdown by political groups. *Source*: VoteWatch Europe.

[...], the new tasks provided for by the Treaty of Lisbon, or unforeseen events, not to mention the political objectives and commitments set by the European council itself."[1] The parliament was also preoccupied about a mounting payment crisis. It feared that the large gap between payments and commitments during 2014–2020 would result in a deficit at the end of cycle.[2]

The European commission proposal

The commission proposed to freeze commitments ceilings at the level corresponding to the final year of the MFF 2007–2013: €1.025bn (2011 prices), ie 1.05 per cent of the EU GNI. With 'special instruments' outside MFF amounting to 0.06 per cent of GNI, the proposal tried to match the parliament's demand for 1.11 per cent.

The commission was more ambitious with regards to shifting spending priorities, arguing that the EU budget should serve the priorities of the Europe 2020 strategy. It pushed for a substantial increase in competitiveness spending (heading 1.a), in particular research and trans-European networks (the connecting Europe facility).[3] By freezing the two largest expenditure items (CAP and cohesion) at 2013 level in current prices, it effectively proposed a real-term decrease in CAP and cohesion spending. It proposed to do so by lowering the ceiling on cohesion spending from four to 2.5 per cent of member states' GNI.[4]

Significantly, the commission also introduced a series of measures to make EU spending more performance-based and more conditional as a way to move further away from 'passive' redistribution. The main measures included 'ex-ante' and 'macroeconomic conditionality'[5] and a performance reserve (to be released only when performance criteria are met) which would apply to structural funds, the extension of 'financial instruments' (ie risk guarantees and loans from a few specific programmes to all funds), environmental conditionality (greening of 30 per cent of the CAP direct payments envelope) and climate mainstreaming (20 per cent of EU spending should serve climate-energy objectives).

Finally, the commission shared the parliament's position on own resources. It proposed to move away from a budget financed primarily by member states' contributions and towards a higher share of 'genuine' own resources, such as a financial transactions tax and a reformed VAT contribution. It also proposed greater transparency by replacing current rebate and correction mechanisms with lump sum reductions.

European council negotiations

After a stage of technical discussions and working groups on the commission's proposal in late 2011 and early 2012, negotiations at European council level only really took off during the Danish presidency in mid-2012. 'Negotiation boxes' were progressively completed under the Danish and Cypriot presidencies, before the council president, Van Rompuy, took over. The first council summit dedicated to the MFF failed to reach an agreement in November 2012. Although already presented with a significant reduction (€970bn, ie €65nn less than the commission proposal), a number of countries, led by the UK but including Sweden, the Netherlands and Denmark, pushed for lowering further the size of the MFF. Other member states, including France and Italy, threatened to use veto if the main headings one and two were further reduced. Indeed, competitiveness expenditure was reduced by 24 per cent from the commission's proposal. It was agreed that further efforts would be pursued to identify potential savings of up to €30bn from other headings, such as administrative expenses. The February 2013 agreement set the level of commitments at €960bn.

Final inter-institutional agreement

In 2013, in contrast to 2006, the parliament did not succeed in challenging MFF ceilings. Faced with the reality of a strong political will in the council behind a real-term reduction in expenditure, it backed down and decided to focus on second-order priorities: flexibility, the mid-term revision clause, own resources and the 'unity' of the budget.[6] It also stressed the importance of solving the issue of payment claims from the 2007–2013 MFF in order to avoid transferring the burden to the new MFF. Following intense negotiations between March and June 2013 (five 'trilogues' at ministerial level, six trilateral meetings at ambassadors' level, and several meetings of the presidents of the three institutions), the parliament and the council reached an agreement. The main results are in line with the parliament's 2011 demands: a compulsory mid-term review with the opportunity for the commission to propose a legislative revision of the MFF by the end of 2016; the setting up of a 'global margin for payments' and a 'global margin for commitments' that would make it possible to shift unused margins from one heading to another; increased carry-over possibilities from one year to the next (put together, these additional flexibilities could give way to an increase in actual spending); and the creation of a high-level group on 'own resources'.

The consent vote in the European parliament took place on 19 November.[7] It was broadly the same configuration as in 2011, with one notable exception: the ECR group voted for, and the Greens against (figure 2.2).

The final outcome shows that the council had the upper hand on the overall amount of spending and headings ceilings (see figure 2.3). The commission did not manage to defend the level of EU spending

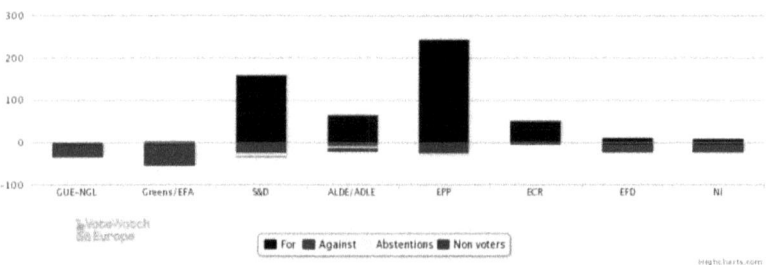

Figure 2.2 European parliament (consent) resolution on the MFF 2014–2020 (November 2013) – Vote breakdown by political groups. *Source*: VoteWatch Europe.

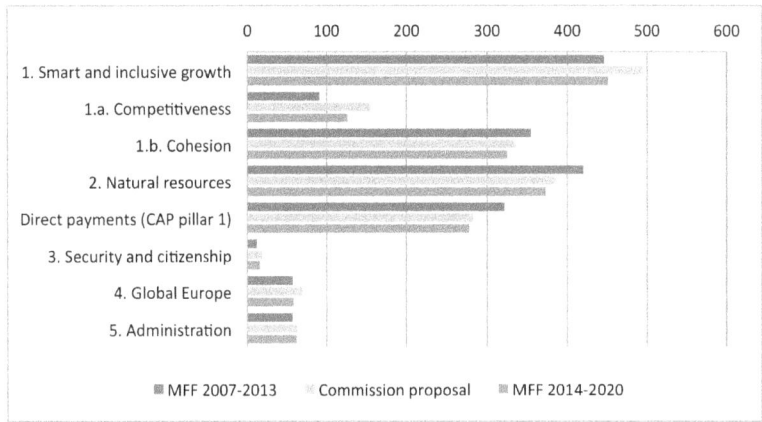

Figure 2.3 Comparison between the MFF 2007–2013, the 2012 commission proposal, and the MFF 2014–2020 (commitment appropriations in €m, 2011 prices).

at its 2013 level, but had some success at streamlining the budget towards the Europe 2020 priorities. The parliament can be credited for pushing the logic of flexibility as far as possible in a pragmatic attempt to make up for spending cuts. In future negotiations, however, MEPs are likely to challenge MFF ceilings again. As the April 2014 parliament resolution on the lessons to be learned from the MFF negotiation put it: "This should by no means be perceived as a precedent and reiterates its position that the MFF figures, and every other part of the European council's relevant political agreement, are subject to negotiations with parliament."[8]

2. POSITIONS AND COALITIONS OF NATIONAL GOVERNMENTS

The net contributory balance of member states, how much they receive in total and what they get from specific budget headings, is central to understanding their positioning in MFF negotiations (see figure 2.4). To the dismay of MEPs and convinced pro-Europeans, budgetary balances, or 'net returns', remains the driving force of

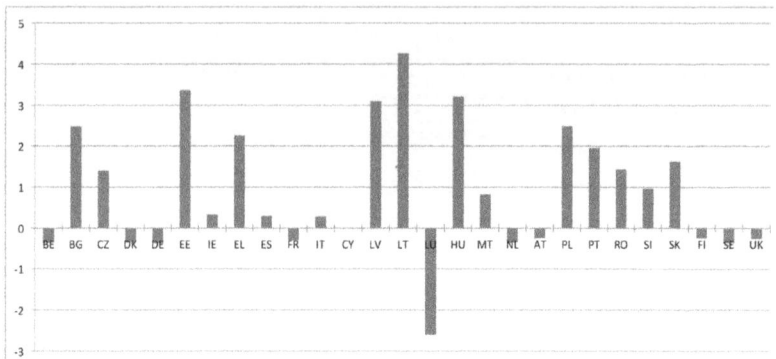

Figure 2.4   Member states budgetary balances, percentage of GNI, 2007–2013 average. *Source*: European commission.

budgetary negotiations, away from the logic of 'European added value'. Net returns may not reflect the holistic benefits of EU spending, such as the acceleration in growth and the improvement in governance in poorer countries and regions, which prevents further economic and social divergence and potential negative spill-overs onto other richer member states.

A further complicating factor behind member states' positioning is that the two largest spending items on the budget, agriculture and structural funds, are calculated in a different way. CAP direct payments go to farmers directly, and thus disproportionally benefit member states with a large farming sector. Structural funds are targeted at the poorest regions, therefore benefiting the least developed countries. As a result, during the last two MFF negotiations, three broad coalitions emerged: 'friends of better spending' (net contributors), 'friends of cohesion' and 'friends of agriculture' (see figure 2.5). These coalitions were not homogenous blocs but their members shared at least one strong preference.

Friends of better spending

This coalition was united by a strong preference for a reduction in overall spending, but did not necessarily agree on the composition of the EU budget. As early as December 2010, before the commission made its proposal, the heads of state and government of five net contributors (the UK, Germany, France, the Netherlands and Finland) asked the commission to freeze payment appropriations at the level of 2011 in real terms in order to support the member states' fiscal consolidation efforts.[9] In November 2012, ahead of the first European council summit dedicated to the MFF, David Cameron lost a vote in the House of Commons on the 'freeze' proposal, leading him to tougher his positon.

Germany and France agreed early on to protect, as far as possible, CAP expenditure. As a result, the UK gave up on pushing for a CAP cut and focused on keeping its rebate. This led the group to target cohesion expenditure, with the view of reducing net contributions and redirecting part of it towards competitiveness.

Friends of cohesion

The coalition brought together the ten central and eastern European member states who joined in 2004 and 2007, and four Mediterranean countries (Greece, Portugal, Spain and Croatia). Throughout 2012, the group organised three high-level meetings, releasing joint statements in favour of maintaining at least current levels of spending on cohesion policy.[10] However, the group's consistency was undermined by differing positions on EU integration, whether or not they were members of the euro, the GNI level (which implies, for some, the likelihood to become net contributors in the next MFF) and the size of the agricultural sector.

As Huza suggests (2014, p.95), the two coalitions' positions were driven not merely by the question of whether they were net contributors or recipients. It also reflects the reality of two different competitiveness models, the 'friends of better spending' relying on high value-added products and services, the 'friends of cohesion' on low-cost strategies. 'Friends of better spending' not only had an interest in capping cohesion money in absolute terms, but also in increasing competitiveness spending since they would be the countries primarily benefitting from it (R&D spending is overwhelmingly absorbed by rich northern and western member states).

Friends of agriculture

Though not a structured coalition like the previous two, a group of member states naturally formed around countries who received a significant share of CAP direct payments, independently of their net position and development level: Poland, France, Romania, Spain, and Ireland. They were supported by a coalition of farmers and environmental NGOs, who defended together the budget allocated to heading two, though not for the same reasons. France played a much more leading role than had been expected considering its negative net position. The French have historically been the main advocate of the CAP.

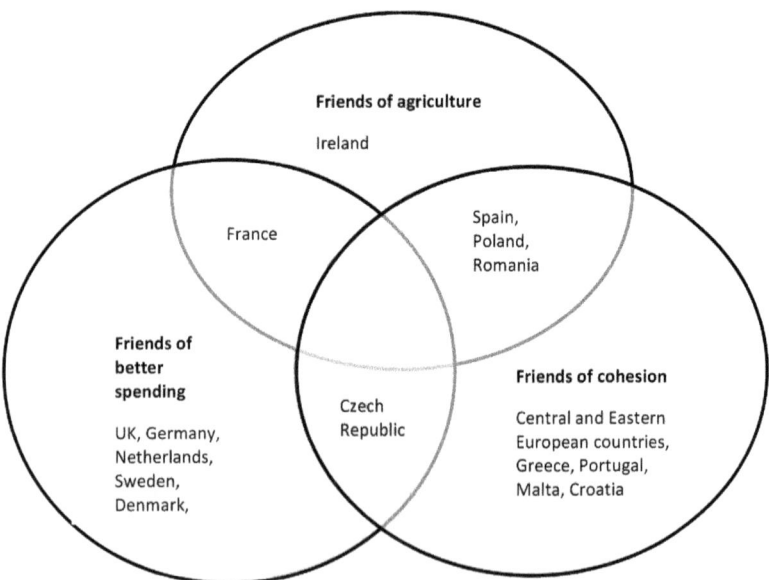

Figure 2.5 **Map of member states positions during the 2014–2020 MFF negotiations.** Own elaboration based on various sources.

Explaining the final outcome

The very strong preference and bargaining power of net contributors in a context of fiscal consolidation is a first explanation for the real term cut in the EU budget despite the cohesion countries' opposition. In January 2012 Germany demanded a 10 per cent cut from the commission proposal at the GAC.[11] In October 2012, the cohesion coalition issued a statement: "There is no room for further reduction following the commission proposal," but they backed down soon after.

Table 2.6 Overview of the positions of Germany, France, Poland and the UK in the MFF negotiation

	Overall level of expenditure	Cohesion	CAP	Other priorities
Germany	Significantly lower	Support to safety net for former convergence regions (German Länder)	Deal with France on freezing CAP direct payments at 2013 level (current prices)	Macroeconomic conditionality of structural funds Research, innovation, education, climate change
France	Lower	Proposed further cuts beyond the Commission's proposal	Despite initial veto threat, accepted to freeze CAP direct payments	Youth employment initiative
Poland	Stable	Diplomatic efforts to manage diverging interests within cohesion group	Stability of direct payments and 'payment convergence' between EU-15 and new member states	
UK	Significantly lower		Strong reduction of CAP budget	Keep the UK rebate

Source: Own elaboration.

Second, the proposal to double-cap cohesion expenditure weakened the 'friends of cohesion' coalition, making the cuts especially acute for the poorest member states. Not only was the cap on cohesion expenditure reduced to 2.35 per cent of member states' GDPs, down from 3.5 per cent over 2007–2013, but member states could not receive more than 110 per cent of what they had received in real terms over 2007–2013.

Third, as a sweetener, 'friends of cohesion' secured a set of favourable conditions for the absorption of cohesion funds, such as extension from two to three years of the maximum execution period, higher co-financing rates, the reimbursement of VAT-related expenses for all projects, facilities for countries under macro-stabilisation programmes, and additional funds for regions with the highest rate of youth unemployment. In addition, safety nets ensured that the regions moving out from the least developed group (formerly 'convergence regions') would still receive at least 60 per cent of their 2007–2013 allocation.

Finally, a decisive factor was that structural funds risked being suspended in absence of an agreement. Unlike CAP direct payments, they do not rely on any treaty obligation and necessitate an agreement.

NOTES

1. "European Parliament resolution of 23 October 2012 in the interests of achieving a positive outcome of the Multiannual Financial Framework 2014–2020 approval procedure." Accessed August 2016, http://www.europarl.europa.eu/sides/getDoc.do?type=TA&reference=P7-TA--0360&language=EN

2. MEPs also claimed that the 2013 EU budget needed to be increased in order to cover the gap between payments and commitments of the present MFF. Finally, in November 2013 the council agreed to cover this gap.

3. "A Budget for Europe 2020." European commission communication, June 29, 2011, COM(2011) 500 final. Accessed August 2016, http://ec.europa.eu/health/programme/docs/maff-2020_en.pdf

4. However a safety net would apply for 'transitions regions' (with a per capita GDP of between 75 per cent and 90 per cent of EU average) to make sure they would still receive at least two-thirds of their structural funds allocation in previous MFF.

5. Ex-ante conditionalities are a prerequisite for efficient use of the ESI Funds. They cover general aspects of a receiving member state's legal environment such as non-discrimination, equal opportunities, public procurement, state aid, efficient public administration, etc. Where the fulfilment of ex-ante conditionalities is not perceived as sufficient, the commission can decide not to pay or to suspend payments. Macroeconomic conditionality establishes a link between ESI funds and the European semester, the EU's main tool of fiscal and macroeconomic coordination. It makes it possible to suspend funds if a member state does not respect its obligations under the excessive deficit procedure and the macroeconomic imbalances procedure.

6. "European Parliament resolution of 13 March 2013 on the European Council conclusions of 7/8 February 2013 concerning the Multiannual Financial Framework." Accessed August 2016, http://www.europarl.europa.eu/sides/getDoc.do?type=TA&language=EN&reference=P7-TA-2013-78

7. "European Parliament legislative resolution of 19 November 2013 on the draft Council regulation laying down the multiannual financial framework for the years 2014–2020." Accessed August 2016, http://www.europarl.europa.eu/sides/getDoc.do?pubRef=-//EP//TEXT+TA+P7-TA-2013-0455+0+DOC+XML+V0//EN

8. "European Parliament resolution of 15 April 2014 on negotiations on the MFF 2014–2020: lessons to be learned and the way forward (2014/2005(INI))." Accessed August 2016, http://www.europarl.europa.eu/sides/getDoc.do?pubRef=-//EP//TEXT+TA+P7-TA-2014-0378+0+DOC+XML+V0//EN

9. "A letter from Prime Minister David Cameron and other European leaders to the President of the European Commission on 18 December 2010." Accessed August 2016, https://www.gov.uk/government/news/letter-to-president-of-european-commission

10. See for instance "Friends of cohesion joint declaration on the Multiannual Financial Framework 2014 – 2020." Accessed August 2016, http://www.vlada.gov.sk/friends-of-cohesion-joint-declaration-on-the-multiannual-financial-framework-2014–2020/

11. Constant Brand, "Germany and UK lead calls for EU spending cuts," *European Voice*, last modified April 12, 2014. Accessed August 2016, http://www.politico.eu/article/germany-and-uk-lead-calls-for-eu-spending-cuts/

THE MFF 2014–2020, TWO YEARS ON

KEY POINTS

- The launch of Jean-Claude Juncker's investment plan for Europe in 2015 has provided a boost to competitiveness spending, though to the detriment of existing research and infrastructure programmes.
- Cohesion policy went through a substantial revamp, not least after the introduction of new conditionalities and instruments common to all European structural and investment funds. Although it is too early to draw lessons from it, this represents a test for the capacity of the EU to spend in a more effective and strategic way.
- The ambition to make the CAP more progressive and green has left many unsatisfied: while some denounce a CAP 'à la carte' lacking ambition, others complain about heavier bureaucracy.
- 'Climate mainstreaming' applies to the whole EU budget, but there is a lack of clarity as to how different programmes and countries are expected to contribute.
- Security, migration and external action spending has been severely impacted by the refugee crisis and terrorism. This has resorted in exceptional measures, in particular the mobilisation of flexibility instruments and the creation of 'trust funds' co-funded by member states.

Beyond the question of the overall ceilings, the MFF negotiations settled the balance between different programmes and set a number of spending rules. This chapter examines the details of the MFF 2014–2020 headings and what can be learned from two years of implementation.

I. COMPETITIVENESS (HEADING I.A): A TIGHT BUDGET FOR HIGH AMBITIONS

The European commission made competitiveness a very clear priority in its 2011 communication *A Budget for Europe 2020*. Though representing only 13 per cent of the budget, competitiveness expenditure was increased by 37 per cent from 2007–2013. The research and development programme Horizon 2020 and the connecting Europe facility (which funds transport, infrastructure and telecommunication networks) benefited from this rise, but both programmes saw the commission's initial ambitions tarnished by the European council. Horizon 2020 must reach a 35 per cent 'climate mainstreaming' target, with research and innovation activities on energy, climate and clean technologies. Other important programmes include Erasmus+ (which encourages students and young professionals' mobility), COSME (which provides support for SMEs) and special projects such as ITER, Galileo and Copernicus.

The creation of the European fund of strategic investments (EFSI) in 2015 by the Juncker commission aimed to mobilise €300bn, mostly from private funding, towards similar objectives. However, Horizon 2020 and CEF envelopes had to be reduced in 2015 and 2016 in order to provide the money for the EFSI guarantee fund. In 2017, the commission proposes to use the global margin for commitments to finance EFSI for up to €1.3bn. By July 2016, it estimated that 50 per cent of the investments approved so far were 'climate-relevant'.[1]

The EFSI raises questions as to its effectiveness and distribution (see assessment by Rubio et al, 2016). Critics emphasise the risk that

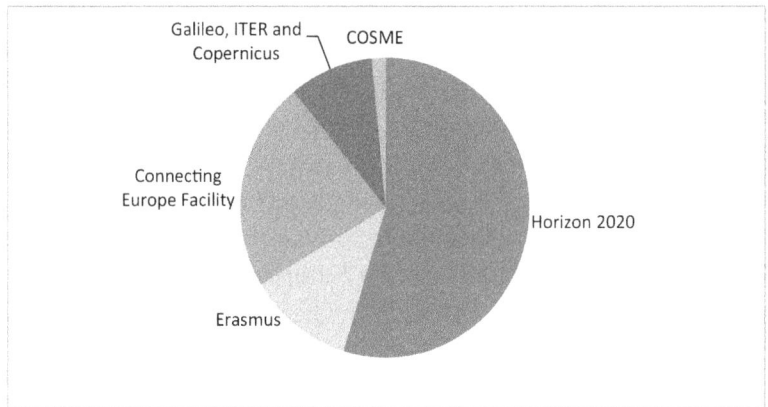

Figure 3.1 Breakdown of competitiveness expenditure by programme. *Source*: European commission.

money goes to investments which would have been financed anyway by national investment banks and/or the European Investment Bank (EIB). The low-carbon content of investment – so far encouraging – is not guaranteed given the short-term, stabilisation rationale behind the creation of EFSI. Finally, EFSI resources seem so far to have benefited a small number of large countries with sophisticated financial markets and experience of EIB investment.

2. COHESION (HEADING 1.B): TRYING NEW APPROACHES

Reorganisation of cohesion policy

On top of an eight per cent real-term cut, cohesion policy went through substantial transformation. Traditionally, its three branches – economic, social and territorial cohesion – corresponded to three distinct funds: the cohesion fund (CF) for the least developed countries, the European social fund (ESF) and the European regional development fund (ERFD). The MFF negotiations led to a reorganisation of spending alongside two main goals. First, 'investment for growth and jobs', covered by the three funds for up to €313bn and designed to support competitiveness objectives; and, second, 'territorial cooperation', covered by the ERDF only (€8bn).

EU money goes to three types of regions, an increase from the two types in the last MFF. 'Less developed regions', with a GDP per capita below 75 cent of the EU average, receive 52 per cent of the total spend and get very favourable co-financing rates from the EU. They include all central and eastern European countries as well as some regions in Portugal, Spain, Italy, Greece and Wales, as well as French and Portuguese overseas territories. Transition regions (GDP per capita between 75 and 90 per cent of the EU average) form a new category which helps soften the transition between less and more developed regions, such as German eastern *L*änder and some French regions. All other regions fall into the 'more developed regions' category and have a GDP per capita above 90 per cent of the EU average.

Besides the three main cohesion funds, the MFF negotiations led to the creation of the €6bn youth employment initiative (YEI). It funds national youth guarantee schemes in regions of high youth unemployment. The decision to front-load commitments in 2014 and 2015 means that most of the available budget has now been spent. Renewing YEI funding will be a key discussion point of the MFF mid-term review, following member states evaluation reports.[2]

New rules and instruments for European structural and investment (ESI) funds

A number of new rules and instruments were attached to all ESI funds, which include the three cohesion policy funds and two 'natural resources' funds (EAFRD and EMFF, see below). The intention was to bring greater strategic consistency between different programmes at national and regional levels as well as to improve the quality and leverage of spending.

– Partnership agreements: In 2014, national (and/or regional) governments had to submit to the commission a list of investment

priorities and actions common to all ESI funds and consistent with the European 2020 strategy, after a consultation with relevant stakeholders and local authorities. It took sometimes up to two years (2014–2015) to finalise partnership agreements and 'operational programmes'.
– Ex-ante conditionalities: Before receiving the money, national or regional authorities need to demonstrate their capacity to manage EU funding and that the right regulatory frameworks are in place.
– Macroeconomic conditionality: ESI funds payments have become conditional on member states' compliance with European semester prescriptions, including recommendations to address 'macroeconomic imbalances'. This mechanism existed in 2007–2013, but it was limited to the excessive deficit procedure.[3] The European parliament reluctantly agreed to what it saw as a punitive and counter-productive approach. However, it caved in after securing a say in any related decision and ensuring that the suspension would be adjusted to social and economic circumstances.
– Climate mainstreaming: 25 per cent of ESI funding must be spent on climate action, though the rate varies across funds and countries. The commission estimates that 16.5 per cent was achieved in 2015.
– Performance reserve: A six per cent reserve can be allocated from 2019 onwards to projects having achieved milestones set for 2018.
– Financial instruments: Compared to 2007–2013, a greater volume of loans, guarantees and equity is available to support investment projects, especially by SMEs, on top of traditional grants. From approximatively €1bn in 2011, the amount spent on financial instruments reached €3bn in 2015.[4] Under certain conditions, a single project can combine financial instruments from both ESI funds and the European fund for strategic investment (see section 1), but this remains complex (Rubio et al, 2016).

Given the significant changes to the structure, rules and tools of cohesion policy, and the delayed completion of 2007–2013 projects, cohesion spending has not yet reached full speed.

3. NATURAL RESOURCES (HEADING TWO): A MORE PROGRESSIVE AND GREEN CAP?

'Natural resources' spending comprises direct payments to farmers and market measures (CAP pillar one), the rural development fund (EAFRD, CAP pillar two), the European maritime and fisheries fund (EMFF) and the programme for the environment and climate action (LIFE+). With a budget of around €3bn, LIFE+ is comparatively small, but its political importance has increased in the context of climate change. Finally, heading two also includes a new reserve for agricultural crises of €2.8bn, the activation of which results in a reduction of direct payments. CAP pillar one was, in relative terms, less impacted by the overall heading two cut.

Cuts in agricultural spending went alongside a revamp of CAP policies. The February 2013 deal on the MFF, and the subsequent CAP reform adopted in October 2013, went some way towards tackling two of the traditional criticisms of the CAP: first, that it does not fund 'public goods' (ie environment and landscape protection) and, second, that it benefits large farms instead of being spent in a more progressive way.

Table 3.2 Evolution of the main sub-headings within heading 2 (€bn, 2011 prices)

	MFF 2007–2013	Commission proposal (2012)	Council agreement (February 2013)	Change (%) from MFF 2007–2013
TOTAL	421	390	373	**-11.3**
CAP Pillar 1 (mostly direct payments)	305	287	278	**-8.8**
CAP Pillar 2 (rural development)	98	84	85	**-13.4**

	2007–2013	2014–2020
LIFE+	€2.1bn (environment only)	€3.5bn, including €2.6bn for the environment and €0.9bn for climate action

Source: IEEP.[1]

[1] IEEP. "A greener EU budget in the balance: the 2014–2020 MFF deal." Accessed August 2016, http://www.ieep.eu/assets/1169/IEEP_Policy_brief_European_Council_agrees_MFF.pdf.

More progressive

Four main measures aim to bring about greater progressivity. These measures do not represent a radical departure, but they mark a new social inflection of CAP's pillar one.

- 'External convergence': Member states with average direct payments per hectare above the EU average see their envelope reduced progressively. Member states with an average direct payment below 90 per cent of the EU average see their allocation go up by one-third by 2020.
- 'Internal convergence': Member states or regions must harmonise the value of basic payments per hectare, or, at least, opt for 'partial convergence'.
- Payment 'degressivity' and 'capping': A five per cent reduction is applied to direct payments above €150,000. Capping direct payments at this level or above is left to the discretion of national governments. The money saved on direct payments is transferred to the rural development national envelope. The attempt, by some member states and the commission, to set up an upper limit to direct payments failed.
- Member states have the option to set up 'redistributive payments' from large to small farms for up to 30 per cent of the national direct payment ceiling.

More green

Advocates of greater environmental conditionality could also register small steps forward. Since 2003, direct payments are conditional on basic 'cross-compliance'. Under the 2014–2020 CAP, cross-compliance is composed of two types of criteria: 'statutory management requirements' (food safety, animal and plant health, animal welfare and environment protection) and 'good agricultural and environmental condition of land' (soil protection, maintenance of soil organic matter and structure, avoiding the deterioration of habitats, and water management). The 'greening' of direct payments agreed upon during the MFF 2014–2020 negotiations represented a further move towards environmental conditionality. Thirty per cent of direct payments are now disbursed only when farms satisfy three requirements as appropriate: the maintenance of permanent grassland, crop diversification and the development of ecological focus areas. All three measures are designed to improve biodiversity records and to help the fight against climate change. By default, organic farms are eligible for green direct payments.

Environmental objectives are also strongly supported by EAFRD, which is channelled through and co-funded by national or regional authorities. As an indication, in 2013, 25 per cent of the EU's utilised agricultural area was under agri-environmental schemes supported by the EAFRD. Over 2014–2020, 30 per cent of the funding should go to environmental and climate projects such as agri-environment management contracts, organic farming, areas of natural constraints, Natura 2000 areas (a network of protected areas made up of sites designated under the Community Birds and Habitats directives), forestry measures and investments. According to a recent study commissioned by the European commission, the EAFRD is the most important ESI fund to support Natura 2000, while integration is much poorer in cohesion policy.[6] However, it is difficult to track Natura 2000 and biodiversity funding in national rural development programmes, and there are no systematic indicators which would make it possible to assess and compare actual progress.

National flexibility and member states choices

The CAP 2014–2020 leaves a lot of flexibility for member states depending on their level of ambition and their priorities, not least the possibility to shift money from one pillar to another ('pillar flexibility'). In 2015, following net transfers made from pillar one to pillar two, the sub-ceiling for direct payments and market-related expenditure went down by €3.5m. As table 3.3 shows, member states have so far had contrasting approaches to the various options available to them. This explains growing criticism of a 'CAP à la carte'.

Table 3.3 How selected member states implement CAP (2014–2020)

	Internal convergence	Degressivity / capping	Redistributive payments (2015–2020)	Flexibility from P1 to P2	Flexibility from P2 to P1
Austria	Full (2019)	Cap at €150,000			
Germany	Full (2015)		7%	4.5%	
France	Partial		From 5% (2015) to 20% (2018)	3.3%	
Ireland	Partial	Cap at €150,000			
Italy	Partial	-50% above €150,000 Cap at €500,000			
The Netherlands	Full (2019)	-5% above €150,000		4.2%	
Poland	n.a.	Capping at €150,000	8.3%		25%
Romania	n.a.	-5% above €150,000 / cap at €300,000	5%	2.1%	
Spain	Partial				
Sweden	Full (2020)	-5% above 150,000			
UK England	Full (2015)	-5% above €150,000		12%	
UK Scotland	Full (2019)	-5% above €150,000 / cap at €500,000		9.5%	

Source: European parliament.[1]
[1] "Implementation of the first pillar of the CAP 2014–2020 in the EU member states." European parliament study, July 2015. Accessed August 2016, http://www.europarl.europa.eu/RegData/etudes/STUD/2015/563386/IPOL_STU(2015)563386_EN.pdf

It may be too early to make an assessment of the CAP 2014–2020 since it took national and regional authorities over a year to integrate new rules (although there have been some early evaluations of greening by the Institute for European Environmental Policy (IEEP) and the commission, see chapter 5). Expected complaints about the new CAP's bureaucratic complexity have led to calls for simplification, something which is likely to dominate the policy review expected in 2017.

In the meantime, several sectors have encountered serious difficulties and necessitated exceptional measures. In particular, the combination of the end of milk quotas in 2015, the Russian embargo on dairy products and declining demand from China have led to a collapse in EU milk prices. The commission was initially reluctant to intervene given the decision taken in 2003 (and confirmed in 2008) to let market mechanisms play their full role. However, some member states like France and Poland urged supply-management measures. In September 2015, a first package of support measures for farmers was announced amounting to €500m. In July 2016, a second package was proposed, which will be enshrined in the EU budget for 2017. In both cases, the money comes from existing envelopes and not from the contingency margin, thus bypassing the risk of a reduction in the overall CAP spend.

4. SECURITY AND CITIZENSHIP (HEADING THREE): THE SHOCK OF THE MIGRATION CRISIS

Heading three covers migration and asylum policy, border management, police and justice cooperation and support to youth and citizenship actions. The two main instruments are the asylum, migration and integration fund (AMIF) and the internal security fund (ISF), representing together about 40 per cent of heading three spending.

When negotiating the MFF in 2011–2013, EU decision-makers could not foresee the dramatic rise in migrants and asylum applications which would shake Europe from 2014 onwards. Nor could they plan for the deterioration in Europe's security environment, especially the rise of Isis terrorism on European soil. Therefore a budget which represents two per cent of the MFF came very quickly under pressure. In 2015 and 2016, exceptional measures were taken to respond to the challenge of the refugee crisis. Funding related to security, border control and migration has doubled over 2015–2016, benefitting in particular three EU agencies (Frontex, the European asylum support office and Europol), the AMIF and the ISF.

Additional resources came from a mix of redeployment of existing funds, using margins and mobilising special instruments (see annex 1 on "Flexibility in the migration crisis" in Mijs and Shout, 2015). A substantial share of these funds is available to support the Greek authorities and international organisations operating in Greece.

In early 2016, the commission proposed the creation of an ad hoc instrument for emergency assistance within the union as a way to "direct humanitarian assistance in EU member states which are experiencing a sudden and massive influx of third-country nationals into their territory." This necessitated the creation of an additional budget of €700m for three years (2016–2018).

The 2017 budget proposal by the commission puts heading three financial needs at €1.8bn higher than that which was initially planned in the MFF.[8] The full mobilisation of the flexibility instrument and the use of the contingency margin will be necessary in the next few years, thus raising the possibility of either decreasing the ceilings in other headings or raising the ceilings during the MFF mid-term review.

5. GLOBAL EUROPE (HEADING FOUR): FINANCIAL INNOVATION IN THE FACE OF NEW CHALLENGES

External action spending features three main instruments targeted at pre-accession countries (IPA), neighbours (ENI), and humanitarian action and development cooperation (DCI). However, instability in Ukraine, Syria and the migration crisis has heavily impacted on the spending structure and led to financial innovation. 'Trust funds' have been established in order to pool large sums of money from public and private actors, including resources from the EU budget's heading four and member states' contributions. The 'Madad fund' (officially the 'regional trust fund in response to the Syrian crisis', benefiting in particular Lebanon, Jordan and Turkey) and the 'EU emergency trust fund for Africa' both aim to provide support to third countries for the management of large migration flows in an instable environment. The 'facility for refugees in Turkey', likewise, mobilises €1bn from the instrument from pre-accession assistance over 2016–2017 and is co-financed by member states. These new initiatives may reflect the limitations of a too-modest EU budget, but they also signal national governments' desire to keep control over sensitive spending areas.

6. ADMINISTRATION (HEADING FIVE): CONTAINMENT OF PERSONNEL AND OPERATIONAL COSTS

Although the share of the MFF allocated to administrative costs has remained stable under the MFF 2014–2020, the European council demanded a five per cent reduction in the staff of all EU institutions and agencies. The resulting increase in working time would not be compensated. This objective is pursued by the commission through cutting its own staff, a containment of external personnel (contract agents, agency staff, local agents and seconded national experts), as well as through a nominal freeze of non-salary expenditure. Some recent decisions have had a financial impact on heading five spending trajectory, such as the chauffeur service now being provided in-house, reinforced security at the European parliament, and the reform of the European court of justice. However, spending is in line with predictions. In 2017, the margin under ceiling available in heading five should be mostly used to offset the use of the contingency margin for heading three.

7. FLEXIBILITY INSTRUMENTS: PROVING THEIR USEFULNESS

The 2007–2013 MFF was criticised for its inflexible character: in the first years, it generated surpluses to be returned to the national budgets, while in the second half the EU budget execution resulted in growing payment deficits that needed to be covered through additional contributions. The European parliament demanded that higher flexibility should be provided for the next period, in particular the possibility of front-loading and back-loading certain budget lines and the use of global margins carryover from one year to another. Though sceptical, the council perceived flexibility as a necessary measure to receive the parliament's consent on an overall reduction in the MFF. Negotiations resulted in the strengthening of existing 'special instruments' siting outside the MFF and the creation and several flexibility instruments.

In a context where any budget revision by more than 0.03 per cent of the EU's GNI requires a joint decision of the parliament and

Table 3.4 Greater flexibility in the use of 'special instruments' outside the MFF

Instrument	Description	Recent use
Emergency Aid Reserve	Up to €280m/year Rapid intervention in non-EU countries	2012: Syria, Mali, Sahel 2016: €150m towards the refugee and migration crisis
Solidarity Fund	Up to €500m/year Emergency aid following a major disaster in a member state	2009: earthquake in Abruzzo 2012: floods in Germany
Flexibility instrument	Up to €471m/year Identified expenses which cannot be covered by the EU budget without exceeding the maximum annual amount for expenditure set out in the MFF.	2014: additional structural funds allocation to Cyprus 2014–2016: full mobilization towards headings 3 and 4 to cope with the migration crisis.
European Globalisation Adjustment Fund	Up to €150m/year Training and active labour market actions after large redundancy plans as a result of major structural changes in world trade patterns	2007–2013: 73 cases and 55,000 dismissed workers targeted over for a total of €187m in a wide range of sectors (food industry, printing, textile, automotive, machinery and equipment, telecommunications, etc.). Re-employment rate is around 50%.

Source: European commission.

Table 3.5 New flexibility instruments under the MFF 2014–2020

Instrument	Description	Implementation so far
Global margin for payments	Unused payment appropriations and margins can be carried over from one financial year to the next. Overall ceiling unchanged.	By the end of the 2014 financial year, €106m were made available again in 2015
Global margin for commitments	Commitment appropriations left unused in 2014–17 will form a reserve for additional expenditure in 2016–20 in the area of growth and employment.	Almost the totality of the global margin for commitments 2014 and 2015 was allocated to the constitution of the EFSI (€543m). A very residual amount was left available in 2016.
Specific flexibility	Provided with the possibility to bring forward expenditure ('frontloading') in 2014/15	€2.1bn frontloaded for the Youth Employment Initiative and up to €400m for research, Erasmus+ and SMEs.
Contingency margin	0.03 % of the EU GNI Last resort instrument to react to unforeseen circumstances	€3.2bn in 2014 to manage the 'payment backlog crisis'. Will have to be offset as from 2018, thus reducing the overall payment ceiling in the MFF last years. For 2017, the Commission proposes to mobilise €1.2bn to reinforce heading 3. Would be offset by tapping into margins under ceilings of heading 2 and 5[1]
Flexibility for aid to the most deprived	Member states can increase their allocation for the aid to the most deprived, yet at the expense of other allocated funds under cohesion policy (heading 1.b).	

Source: European commission.
[1] "Draft EU budget proposal for 2017. General Introduction." *ibid*.

council, special instruments are a flexibility instrument as such. The 2014–2020 inter-institutional agreement provides for greater flexibility in their use and mobilisation with a view to having sufficient resources to cope with all underlying unforeseen events.

Tables 3.4 and 3.5 show that extensive use has been made of all internal and external flexibility instruments since 2014. In 2015, in its resolution on the council position on the draft budget for 2016, the European parliament deplored that "barely two years after the beginning of the current MFF, the commission has had to twice request the mobilisation of the flexibility instrument, as well as the deployment of the contingency margin, in order to cover pressing and unforeseen needs that could not be financed within the existing MFF ceilings." Whether the EU budget needs larger flexibility instruments or higher ceilings will be a question at the heart of the MFF mid-term review.

NOTES

1. "Accelerating Europe's transition to a low-carbon economy." European commission communication, July 20, 2016, COM(2016) 500 final. Accessed August 2016 https://ec.europa.eu/transparency/regdoc/rep/1/2016/EN/1-2016-500-EN-F1-1.PDF, 6

2. "Draft EU budget proposal for 2017. General Introduction." Accessed August 2016, http://ec.europa.eu/budget/biblio/documents/2017/2017_en.cfm, 25

3. It was only applied once, when the council suspended some commitments from the cohesion fund to Hungary. See "The European Structural and Investment Funds." European parliament briefing, July 2015. Accessed August 2016, http://www.europarl.europa.eu/RegData/etudes/BRIE/2015/565873/EPRS_BRI(2015)565873_EN.pdf, 5

4. "Consolidated annual accounts of the European Union 2015." European commission communication, July 11, 2016, COM(2016) 475 final, Accessed August 2016, http://ec.europa.eu/budget/library/biblio/documents/2015/EU_AnnualAccounts2015_EN.pdf

5. IEEP. "A greener EU budget in the balance: the 2014–2020 MFF deal." Accessed August 2016, http://www.ieep.eu/assets/1169/IEEP_Policy_brief_European_Council_agrees_MFF.pdf

6. European commission / N2K, "Integration of Natura 2000 and biodiversity into EU funding (EAFRD, ERDF, CF, EMFF, ESF). Analysis of a selection of operational programmes approved for 2014–2020." European commission, 2016. Accessed August 2016, http://ec.europa.eu/environment/nature/natura2000/financing/docs/Natura2000_integration_into_EU%20funds.pdf

7. "Implementation of the first pillar of the CAP 2014–2020 in the EU member states." European parliament study, July 2015. Accessed August 2016, http://www.europarl.europa.eu/RegData/etudes/STUD/2015/563386/IPOL_STU(2015)563386_EN.pdf

8   "Draft EU budget proposal for 2017. General Introduction." *op. cit.*, 3.

WHAT CAN BE EXPECTED FROM THE MFF MID-TERM REVIEW?

KEY POINTS

- The MFF mid-term review is highly constrained by a limited timeframe, a low appetite for shaking the fragile equilibrium reached in 2013, and the freeze of national envelopes including structural funds and the CAP direct payments.
- The European parliament is pushing for higher ceilings in the face of new pressures, especially insecurity and instability in the EU's neighbourhood. However, the outcome is likely to be greater flexibility under existing ceilings and outside the MFF.
- Within the MFF, the carrying over of annual surpluses and the use of all available margins will be pushed to its limits. Outside the MFF, member states will pursue the development of co-financed 'trust funds' or 'facilities' and push for the relaxation of state spending limits, for instance in agriculture.
- Strikingly, although the December 2015 Paris climate agreement is perceived as significantly raising the stakes for the EU, the MFF mid-term review is unlikely to channel more resources towards environmental objectives.

I. A SQUEEZED PROCESS WITH A LIMITED SCOPE

The MFF regulation (article 2) stipulates that the European commission "shall present a review of the functioning of the MFF" and "as appropriate, a legislative proposal for a revision of the MFF regulation" by no later than the end of 2016 (see figure 4.1). It is, therefore, not legally obliged to table a legislative proposal. Since the commission is legally bound to present a legislative proposal for the post-2020 MFF before 1 January 2018, this leaves a short window for any (mid-term revision) legislative process to take place. In addition, sectoral policies will also be submitted to a mid-term evaluation, which is expected to take place in the first half of 2017. With strong interlinks between the budget and individual policies, it is necessary to consider both aspects as part of the mid-term review.

The addition of a 'review/revision' clause to the MFF regulation was a key European parliament demand. The main rationale behind it was to ensure that the newly installed EU institutions (especially

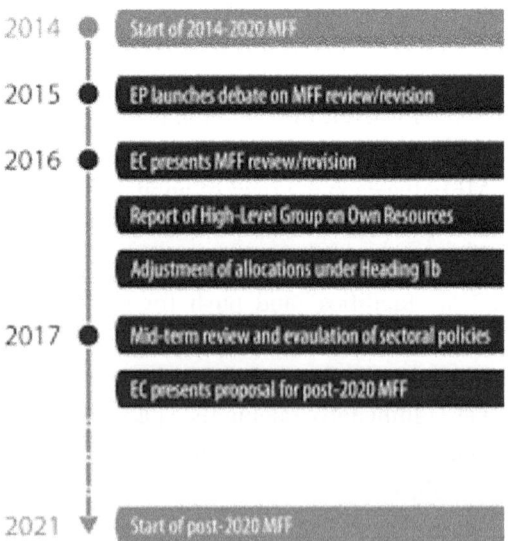

Figure 4.1 Timeline of the mid-term review/revision of the MFF. *Source*: European parliament[1].

after the May 2014 European parliamentary elections) would be able to reassess the EU's political priorities and endow the MFF with renewed democratic legitimacy. The parliament is thus the most vocal actor behind the idea of a fully fledged revision.

The 2007–2013 precedent does not suggest that the upcoming review will bring about substantial changes in the MFF. The final agreement on the MFF 2007–2013 provided for "a full, wide-ranging review covering all aspects of EU spending, including the CAP, and of resources, including the UK rebate."[2] However, the review was delayed until late 2010 due to the financial crisis, the ratification of the Lisbon treaty and the 2009 European parliament elections. The launch of the Europe 2020 strategy also prompted the commission and parliament to focus on the next MFF. The review, therefore, proved to be a mere preparatory exercise for the MFF 2014–2020 and did not bring about any significant changes to the MFF 2007–2013.

However, the legal context was different. The MFF 2007–2013 was revised four times before the review, for instance in order to secure funding for projects such as Galileo and Iter. In an interview for this project, an experienced diplomat observed that the post-Lisbon revision procedure is less flexible. Any MFF revision now requires unanimity, while previously it necessitated only a qualified majority when its impact was on less than 0.03 per cent of the EU GNI.

The commission is expected to launch the review in the early autumn. The standard view among government officials close to the dossier is that the review can only achieve limited results given both a window of three months (September–December) and the difficult political context. They stress that 'national' envelopes (ie all ESI funds, direct payments and some heading three funds under shared management such as AMIF and ISF) are ring-fenced, and that there is no appetite to reopen discussions on ceilings. The Brexit context casts a new shadow on the review and may prompt extra caution about any suggestion to spend more or any move which could upset electorates.

In practice, any legislative proposal by the commission is likely to take the form of an 'omnibus' regulation. Instead of amending dozens of regulations linked to specific funds or programmes, a series of technical adjustments in different areas would be put forward in a single package. This would speed up and centralise the process since the draft legislation would be discussed in the general affairs council (ie foreign affairs or Europe ministers) and not in different council formats. It would also facilitate informal 'trilogue' negotiations between the commission, the council and the parliament. Such an option would probably mean a streamlined process centred around big, urgent matters.

2. KEY THEMES AND IDEAS PUT FORWARD BY EU INSTITUTIONS

European parliament

In December 2015, the committee on budgets launched a discussion, which led to the adoption in July 2016 of a resolution "on the preparation of the post-electoral revision of the MFF 2014–2020."[3] The resolution was prepared by rapporteurs Jan Olbrycht (Germany, EPP) and Isabelle Thomas (France, S&D). It was adopted by a large majority bringing together the centre right, centre left, liberals and greens.

The resolution paints a very bleak picture. It stresses the unexpected impact of the refugee crisis, a persistently high level of youth unemployment, new security threats, and the ongoing difficulties faced by farmers. All of this has resulted in the exhaustion of "all available margins" and a "substantial use" of flexibility provisions. The resolution also warns against a new payments crisis in the making. As a consequence, it sees a revision of the MFF regulation as "absolutely indispensable if the union is to effectively confront a number of challenges while fulfilling its political objectives," especially delivering the goals of Europe 2020 strategy.

In private, MEPs are realistic about their chances of influencing the council's position on ceilings given national red lines and the fact that most cohesion and CAP money is ring-fenced. Nevertheless, the parliament demands the upward revision of commitment ceilings in four areas:

- Heading 1.a: Offset the EFSI-related cuts affecting Horizon 2020 and the CEF.
- Heading 1.b: Continue to finance the youth employment initiative.
- Heading three: Reinforce the AMIF and the ISF, which are both impacted by the creation of the new emergency assistance instrument, as well as by new initiatives such as the European border and coast guard agency and the 'Dublin III' regulation recast.
- Heading four: Cover the increasing needs related to the external dimension of the refugee and migration crisis without hampering existing programmes.

In order to avoid a new payment crisis, the parliament demands a corresponding upwards revision of payments ceilings. Other suggested technical improvements include the "automatic transfer to the following years of any surplus resulting from under-implementation […] or fines imposed on companies," and the lifting of any restriction on the use of flexibility instruments in order to allow for a "maximum use of the global MFF ceilings for commitments and payments." The parliament proposes to push the emergency aid reserve and the flexibility instrument up to €1bn and €2bn respectively. Finally, it observes that "an increasing use of financial instruments (ie loans and guarantees rather than grants and subsidies) should not lead to a reduction in the union budget."

The resolution is a compromise between different political forces and parliamentary committees. Table 4.2 gives an overview of the concerns and demands of the parliament's sectoral committees as expressed in their contributions to the resolution. Unsurprisingly, each committee defends its own turf. The defensive tone of the agriculture committee's opinion, by far the longest contribution, is particularly striking. By contrast, the environment committee stressed the rationale for adapting the budget to the post-Paris/COP 21 context.

Table 4.2 Main concerns and demands from EP committees for the MFF mid-term review

Committee	Analysis	Main demands
Industry, Transport, Research and Enterprise (ITRE) Regional Development	EFSI investment does not substitute for Horizon 2020 and CEF projects Limited evidence available - early stage of implementation of ESI funds Need for greater simplicity and synergies among funds, programmes and financial instruments	Incorporate EFSI into the EU budget "without any negative financial impact" Provide additional assistance to states and regions "providing appropriate reception conditions and integration asylum seekers and other migrants"
Employment and Social Affairs (EMPL)	Warns against a deteriorated social situation	Fund the Youth Employment Initiative until 2020 Equip EURES and new platform against undeclared work with proper funding Instore a Child guarantee "with dedicated special resources, together with programmes to assist parents in getting out of social exclusion and unemployment"
Environment, Public Health and Food Safety (ENV)		Adapt the MFF to achieve the goals of the Paris climate agreement "Sufficient resources in the upcoming budgets" to preserve biodiversity, esp. "an adequate budget and financing for the Natura 2000 network, in particular through the LIFE programme"

Agriculture (AGRI)	The CAP is "cheap," has a low error rate and fulfils a broad range of objectives, including sustainability Cuts in direct payments from last MFF negotiations make it difficult to cope with price volatility	Heading 2 "must remain at least at the same level," including direct payments, in order to meet "the ever-increasing challenges faced by the CAP" Keep two-pillar structure and a "well-functioning, well-financed second pillar" Adequate compensation measures to deal with unforeseen events and market failures
Civil Liberties, Justice and Home Affairs (LIBE)	MFF ceilings, esp. heading 3, "have proven to be too tight" Concern over the Refugee facility for Turkey (use and unicity of the budget)	"Substantial additional financial resources," especially for AMIF and EASO Create dedicated 'search and rescue fund' instead of taking from the ISF
Foreign Affairs	EU faced with "an unprecedented number of crises" [...] "unforeseen at the time the MFF was concluded" Multiplication of facilities and trust funds outside the EU budget bad for transparency and accountability	Raise payments and commitments ceilings under heading 4 "A substantial reform of the flexibility mechanisms under the MFF, setting up a permanent system that allows for the mobilisation of additional resources when needed" Possibility to transfer funds between headings

Source: European parliament.

Finally, the main political groups have contributed to the mid-term review preparatory debates. In their position papers, the three centrists groups (EPP, S&D, ALDE) agree the necessity of revising the ceilings of headings 1.a, three and four upwards, and of continuing to fund the youth employment initiative. They all call for preventive action in order to avoid another payment crisis by the MFF. Laying the groundwork for the post-2020 MFF, they demand respect for the unity of the budget (that is, avoiding the multiplication of special instruments outside the MFF) and a genuine system of own resources. They are all in favour of the alignment of the MFF duration with the political cycle of the parliament and the commission.

There are some slight nuances when going into details. The S&D group demands an upward revision of heading 1.b spending with, in particular, the establishment of a new specific fund dedicated to a European child guarantee and an increase in the ESF and the FEAD. Social democrats are also critical of the commission's "fuzzy and unambitious solutions" in the face of new constraints. They hit out at the rhetoric of 'better spending' and sound a note of scepticism on the vague concept of 'European added value'.

In their amendments presented in the budgets committee, the Greens proposed to raise the level of climate-related expenditure from 20 to 30 per cent in the wake of the Paris climate deal. They also suggested scrapping Iter and pushed for a "maximalist approach of the revision of the MFF [...] up to the own resources ceiling (1.23 per cent of the EU GNI in payments) which would roughly lead to an additional €120bn."

European commission

Up to July 2016, the European commission has said very little about its intentions with regard to the mid-term review. The webpage dedicated to the MFF on the commission's website merely features Juncker's statement in his July 2014 speech to the European parliament on 'political guidelines for the next European commission':

> "The mid-term review of the MFF, scheduled for the end of 2016, should be used to orient the EU budget further towards jobs, growth and competitiveness."

The review was mentioned in the commission's work programme for 2016, which was published in October 2015.[4]

> "The mid-term review of the MFF will look at how better to target funding on the priorities we face, such as the internal and external dimensions of the refugee crisis. Furthermore the commission will propose a strategy on 'an EU budget focused on results' to ensure that future financing has a stronger focus on achieving results. More can be done to facilitate the use of innovative financial instruments, and there is considerable scope for simplification (in particular in agriculture, the ESI funds and further efforts on research), performance-enhancement and measures linking effectiveness of funds to sound economic governance."

In December 2015, the commission released an indicative roadmap on the mid-term review "communication and proposal" to be presented in 2016.[5] The roadmap mentions "relevant inputs" such as the first evaluation of the youth employment initiative, the recommendations from the high-level group on simplification of the ESI funds and the first outputs of the budget focused on results strategy. It suggests that the review will pay particular attention to the functioning of the global margins for payments and commitments, Horizon 2020 funding and the duration of the MFF, as well as to "systemic shortcomings of the EU budget."

In September 2015, the EU budget commissioner, Kristalina Georgieva, launched the 'EU budget focused on results' initiative as a way to focus attention on the quality rather than on the volume of spending. The initiative looks at four areas: the added value of the EU budget (ie whether money allocation is allocated in a way which generates greater returns than if it was done at national level); the way in which money is spent (especially the scope for flexibility, financial instruments and conditionality); the methods for assessing spending; and better communication with the public. In a speech at a conference organised by the Dutch presidency in Amsterdam in January 2016, the commissioner dropped a few hints at the technical adjustments and questions which would be discussed during the review:[6]

- More money will be necessary to "accommodate the needs to address the refugee crisis - internally and partially externally." However, this may be done by bringing about "synergies and interoperability across current headings."
- Should new tools such the Turkey facility and the trust fund for Syria, be brought into the EU budget or left outside?
- Are the greening of the CAP and macroeconomic conditionality working?

In private, senior commission officials confirm that greater budget flexibility in order to address the refugee crisis will be the main thrust of the review. They acknowledge that headings three and four are too low, but stress that several options are available to address this situation, some being "more controversial" than others. They also underline the political constraints surrounding the mid-term review and the fact that the 2014–2020 programmes have only just started to be implemented. On the CAP, limited technical adjustments are expected to take place, such as leaving more flexibility to the member states on the 'active farmer' definition, extending the use of financial instruments in rural development, and expanding 'ecological focus areas' – one of the three qualifying criteria for green payments – from five to seven per cent of holdings' arable area.

Council – Dutch presidency (January-June 2016)

The EU budget has featured highly in the Dutch presidency's agenda. 'Sound European finances' was one of its four priorities. The January Amsterdam conference on the EU budget was a way to prepare the ground for the MFF mid-term review as well as, according to a Dutch official, "break away from the MFF legacy and promote new ideas and methods." It originated in a pledge made by former foreign minister Frans Timmermans after what was perceived to be a disappointing result from the MFF negotiations in 2013.

The 'Amsterdam map' published after the conference provides a number of ideas "on the principles that could guide the future MFF." However, it does not explicitly mention the mid-term review.[7] In April, the Dutch government hosted two informal general affairs council (GAC) and economic and financial affairs council (Ecofin) meetings to discuss the review and the Amsterdam map. A few options for greater budget flexibility were discussed at the Ecofin meeting, especially carrying over the annual surpluses and the unused contingency margin from one year to another, as well as using fines collected by the European commission. Ministers also suggested that the use of 'trust funds' needed to be regularised. These adjustments are expected to be part of the financial regulation presented by the commission in the autumn.

3. ATTITUDES IN KEY EU GOVERNMENTS AND PARLIAMENTS

Germany: tackle new priorities through greater flexibility

Germany was broadly satisfied with the MFF negotiations results. Key demands such as the EU budget's cap at one per cent of the EU GNI and the introduction of macroeconomic conditionality were adopted. From an environmental perspective, CAP greening was seen as a first step in the right direction.

Expectations with the mid-term review are low in Berlin. According to a senior diplomat, it will "not include any numbers" and a ground-breaking outcome is unlikely given that pressure to compromise will be low. Like Georgieva, the German government does not see the tightness of the EU budget as necessarily a bad thing. However, they strongly advocate greater flexibility as a way to enhance the EU's capacity for action and to cope with a more volatile and uncertain environment.

German officials are, therefore, interested in the possibility of shuffling more resources towards headings three and four, but also of mobilising further 'special instruments' outside the MFF. Channelling more money towards the new European border and coast guard agency is a priority. A new idea mentioned by German policymakers is the creation of a dedicated fund for the integration of refugees. Extra resources would come from financial penalties related to the misuse of CAP direct payments, which are currently under the control of the agriculture council.

Changes to the CAP, however, are not seen as likely in the short term, nor are the new Paris climate objectives seen as a reason to dramatically increase environmental funding. A spokesperson of an environmental charity said he had little hope that the MFF mid-term review would substantially change the CAP rules. However he pointed to the possibility of this happening via the REFIT platform chaired by the commission's first vice-president, Timmermans (see chapter 5 section on CAP reform).

France: security concerns dominate

The French government is cautious when it comes to EU budget discussions. The MFF was negotiated at the time of the French 2012 presidential elections. The Socialist win against Nicolas Sarkozy resulted in a slight shift of the French position towards greater support for growth and cohesion measures and less support for overall cuts. Given its defensive attitude on the CAP and a difficult budgetary situation, the French government could not obtain everything it was asking for. A series of symbolic pay-offs, such as the youth employment initiative and the maintenance of the food programme (a fund providing European aid to the most deprived) helped François Hollande pitch the outcome as a success.

Like the attitude of their German colleagues, French policymakers do not see the MFF mid-term review as moment for significant change, but rather for technical adjustments. They stress that, in a context of dire public finances, "the overall ceilings are taboos" and that pre-allocated national envelopes will not be revised. Nevertheless, they admit that more money is needed in headings three and four. A "security pact" and the financing of the new European border and coast guard agency are mentioned. In a joint statement with his counterpart Franz-Walter Steinmeier on 27 June 2016, French foreign minister Jean-Marc Ayrault set out a vision for the future of the EU centred around three priorities: a security compact, a common asylum and migration policy, and the completion of economic and monetary union.

The mid-term review is not seen as an opportunity to reopen the CAP rules. French officials stress that there should only be secondary legislation changes in the mid-term (policy) review of the CAP since the rules are new and were negotiated for seven years. They accept that the new CAP would benefit from simplification and point out that the commission is currently undertaking an evaluation of greening. However, the government defends the very principle of greening and would not be opposed to the extension of ecological focus areas from five to seven per cent – something which needs to be decided in 2017.

Poland: defending the status quo

The Polish government is broadly satisfied with the MFF and the substantial shares allocated to cohesion and agriculture. Polish officials stress that the MFF has already changed a lot, for instance with the extension of financial instruments (which mostly benefit wealthier countries). The mid-term review will "not be a time to reopen everything." Poland is realistic that "net payers will not agree on raising ceilings." At best, it is a moment to improve the way in which flexibility operates and to address the gap between commitments and payments.

The Polish view is that CAP pillar one is part of the 'pre-allocated national envelopes' and therefore cannot be affected by the mid-term review. Poland has already been pushing for a simplification of direct payment rules: in May 2016, the Polish agriculture ministry issued a paper, which recommends applying sanctions against "minor non-compliance" in a more proportionate way, "unburdening the on-the-spot check process" and "mitigating the approach to excluding EFAs if they exceed the size specified in the provisions." Poland will therefore closely follow the evaluation of greening and oppose any higher environmental ambition unless there is sufficient flexibility.

UK: low profile ahead of Brexit negotiations

For obvious reasons the UK government is not expected to throw its weight behind the MFF mid-term review. If anything, one can expect it to oppose any raise in ceilings and national contributions.

The Netherlands: throw in new ideas for the post-2020 EU budget

During the last MFF negotiations, the Dutch government pursued the objective of a budget of less than one per cent of the EU GNI and the end of cohesion spending in rich countries. The outcome of the negotiations proved disappointing. Dutch policymakers were also upset by the €642m 'surcharge' requested by the commission in October 2014, when the Netherlands, like the UK, saw its GNI and its contribution to the EU revised upwards. Although expectations are low for the mid-term review, the Netherlands used their presidency of the EU in the first half of 2016 to promote the vision of a more transparent and flexible budget, and open debates about the post-2020 MFF.

NOTES

1. "Mid-term review/revision of the MFF Key issues at the outset of the debate." European parliament briefing, January 2016. Accessed August 2016, http://www.europarl.europa.eu/RegData/etudes/BRIE/2016/573952/EPRS_BRI(2016)573952_EN.pdf

Table 4.3 Summary of member states positions regarding the MTR of the MFF

	Expectations	Priority	Agriculture and environment
Germany	More flexibility without raising the ceilings	More money for border surveillance, migrants integration	Little room for manoeuvre given coalition agreement
France	More flexibility without raising the ceilings	Security pact Youth Employment Initiative	Against revision of basic CAP rules but open to secondary legislation changes
Poland	Status quo	Avoid expansion of financial instruments	Strong push for lighter controls on farmers
UK	Low priority	Prepare Brexit talks in good conditions	Uncertainty about CAP and structural funds after Brexit
Netherlands	Advance vision of a radical EU budget reform	Competitiveness	Less bureaucracy on small farms and entrepreneurs

Source: Own elaboration.

2. "Financial Perspective 2007–2013." Council of the European Union, Note 15915/05, December 19, 2005. Accessed August 2016, http://www.consilium.europa.eu/ueDocs/cms_Data/docs/pressData/en/misc/87677.pdf, 32

3. "Report on the preparation of the post-electoral revision of the MFF 2014–2020: Parliament's input ahead of the Commission's proposal, (2015/2353(INI))." June 30, 2016. Accessed August 2016, http://www.europarl.europa.eu/sides/getDoc.do?pubRef=-%2f%2fEP%2f%2fTEXT%2bREPORT%2bA8-2016-0224%2b0%2bDOC%2bXML%2bV0%2f%2fEN&language=EN

4. "Commission Work Programme 2016. No time for business as usual." European commission communication. October 27, 2015, COM(2015) 610 final. Accessed August 2016, http://ec.europa.eu/atwork/pdf/cwp_2016_en.pdf, 4

5. "Roadmap for the Commission communication and proposal for a Council regulation on the mid-term review of the MFF 2014–2020." European commission, December 2015, Accessed August 2016, http://ec.europa.eu/smart-regulation/roadmaps/docs/2016_sg_003_mff_2014-2020_en.pdf

6. "Outcomes of the EU conference on the Multiannual Financial Framework (MFF)." The Netherlands EU presidency 2016. February 26, 2016, https://english.eu2016.nl/latest/news/2016/02/26/outcomes-of-the-eu-conference-on-the-multiannual-financial-framework-mff

WHAT WILL THE EU BUDGET LOOK LIKE AFTER 2020? WHAT FUTURE FOR THE CAP?

KEY POINTS

- The political context in which the next MFF negotiations will take place will mean that any ambition to shake up radically EU budget conservatism will not necessarily mean transferring more money to the EU. Instead, achieving 'more with less' will become a mantra in an EU increasingly controlled by national governments.
- There will be strong arguments for greater macroeconomic and green conditionality in the context of eurozone governance reforms and the EU's climate-energy commitments.
- In exchange, the EU will have to become less intrusive. A contractual approach could dominate ESI funds and the CAP, whereby national and regional actors submit local plans to achieve EU targets.

1. THREE POST-2020 EU BUDGET SCENARIOS

There are lots of unknowns about the future of the EU budget. How will Brexit impact on the timing and key member states' positions? Can negotiations really start before Britain actually leaves and before a new European parliament and a new commission take office in 2019? Will the current wave of Euroscepticism across member states prompt national leaders to push for a more ambitious EU budget, including higher own resources, a eurozone budget and more resources for investment? Or will it lead to further caution and another attempt to deflate the EU budget?

What we know is that the European commission must present a proposal before 1 January 2018. Discussions are therefore expected to start in the course of 2017. If the UK activates Article 50 in early 2017, the compensation for the loss of the UK's annual net contribution (£8.5bn/€11bn in 2015) will be part of the MFF negotiations. Finally, not only figures but policies are at stake. The debate on the future of the CAP and cohesion policy has already started and will be held in parallel to the MFF negotiations.

The Juncker commission is unlikely to put forward a proposal which member states are likely to reject. Georgieva calls the current equilibrium "financial peace." Previous MFF negotiations saw ambitious commission proposals thwarted by member states. The more political approach of the current commission means that they will make substantial reform proposals only if they are confident that large member states are supportive. In her January 2016 Amsterdam speech, Georgieva acknowledged that both approaches had their merits and rationale:[1]

> "There are two schools of thought about the future MFF. The first school says that we need a radical change of the structure of the EU budget to respond to the priorities in this fast changing world – this would mean departing from the current equilibrium towards a new one. This will be a risky and uncertain enterprise but perhaps a necessary one. The second school says that the next MFF should keep the current equilibrium and follow the path of the current MFF to continue the process of gradual improvements as I have highlighted above: increasing the share of projects with a high EU added value, increasing performance, flexibility and the use of financial instruments, etc."

History teaches that the EU budget only changes incrementally given the number of players involved you can use their veto. The current sentiment of existential crisis and the need to make change visible might nevertheless encourage leaders to show more ambition. However, ambition can mean different things. Table 5.1 suggests three theoretical scenarios: incremental change, a more ambitious approach with more EU resources, and a more ambitious approach with fewer resources.

2. EARLY INDICATIONS OF MEMBER STATES' POSITIONING

It is impossible to predict what the exact positions of key member states will be in 2018 and 2019, all the more so since major elections are due to take place in 2017 in France, the Netherlands, Germany, and the political situation in Spain, Italy and Austria is uncertain. However, some assumptions are possible from a series of factors.

First, few countries are likely to change radically their position from the MFF 2013–2020 negotiations. A decisive factor determining member states' positioning is their net balance. A few fast-growing countries like Czech Republic, Slovakia and the Baltic countries are likely to become net contributors over time, something they already anticipated in the last negotiations. However, the clash between contributors and beneficiaries is likely to happen again. Informal consultations are taking place between 'friends of better spending' and 'friends of cohesion'.

Second, the aftermath of the British referendum and the central position acquired by Eurosceptic and anti-EU parties in the last few years means that transferring a higher share of national resources to the EU level is unlikely. Agreeing on new tax resources for the EU – something which the Monti report due in December 2016 might recommend – will be extremely difficult since it necessitates member states giving away crucial fiscal resources. At best, there will only be symbolic moves in this direction.

Third, the discussions of the MFF mid-term review set the tone. The critical questions could be formulated as such: how to achieve

Table 5.1 Three theoretical scenarios for the post-2020 EU budget

	Incremental change	More with more	More with less
Overall volume	Stability	+ 10–20% and/or Eurozone fiscal capacity	Stability or decrease
Duration	7 years (2021–2027)	5 years (2021–2026) or 5+5 (mid-term review after 5 years)	5 years (2021–2026) or 5+5 (mid-term review after 5 years)
Own resources	No change – compensation for the UK's net contribution	Follow up on High level group on own resources recommendations	No change – compensation for the UK's net contribution
Eurozone budget and governance	Reinforced macroeconomic conditionality of EU funding	Eurozone budget, for instance investment facility compensating for structural reforms	Reinforced macroeconomic conditionality of EU funding
Competitiveness	Slight increase Extension of the Investment plan for Europe (EFSI) more financial instruments	Substantial increase	
Cohesion	Freeze or slight decrease Expansion of financial instruments and performance-based budgeting	Slight decrease Less money towards rich regions Child guarantee fund (Youth Employment Initiative model)	Sharp decrease No money towards rich regions Expansion of financial instruments and performance-based budgeting

CAP and environment	Freeze or slight decrease Better coverage of price volatility risk and/or more room for state subsidies and 'coupled support' More flexible approach to greening	Stabilisation 50 per cent climate mainstreaming; expand greening + more resources for green investment	Sharp decrease Cap of direct payments or income insurance More flexible approach to greening More resources for green investment, esp. through financial instruments
Security, migration, external affairs	Slight increase	Substantial increase	
Flexibility	Continuation with likely outcome of MFF mid-term review	Reintegration of trust funds and facilities into MFF Unused money systematically returns to MFF Larger Contingency margin and Flexibility instrument	Maximal, eg flexibility between headings at EU and national level

Source: Own elaboration.

better results with less money and less intrusive or rigid rules and whether the EU can be reinforced without giving away too much power and resources to Brussels. Centre-right and centre-left governments are desperate to demonstrate the EU's added value and relevance, but they know that giving new financial and institutional resources to the EU is politically very risky.

For all these reasons, those who dream of a radical increase or restructuring of the EU budget may have to wait once again. The following section provides an overview of German (and Dutch), French and Polish expectations and priorities. It is based on interviews conducted for this research.

Germany (and Netherlands): more with less

- The budget freeze at one per of the EU's GNI should continue unless the fiscal situation and public sentiment toward the EU in member states radically improves.
- A budget of investment and the extension of financial instruments: The EFSI is seen as a possible way forward for a larger chunk of the EU budget. German officials think an investment-orientated budget should become the rule across headings one and two, either by focusing direct payments and grants on growth-enhancing measures or by extending the use of financial instruments, especially in rich regions. The German ministry for agriculture is interested in the idea of a more investment-orientated CAP, while partially making income support a national responsibility.
- More European added value and performance-based budgeting: In a speech in September 2015, the German finance minister, Wolfgang Schäuble, stressed that 70 per cent of the EU budget was currently used to "replace national spending," mainly on the basis of "historical reasons." Strategic priorities where spending have real added value included migration, foreign affairs, the environment, energy and the digital transition.[2] Dutch officials are worried about weak absorption capacity and the lack of clear European added value to some projects. Germany and the

Netherlands both strongly back the commission's 'EU budget for results' initiative. Finance ministries in these countries are likely to put 'better spending' at the core of their strategy during the next MFF negotiations, although, in practice, the end result is subject to arbitration between different ministries and political forces.
– Tougher macroeconomic conditionality of structural funds: In 2011–2013, Germany pushed for the introduction of 'ex-ante conditionalities' and 'macroeconomic conditionality'. This was a first step to establishing a link between European semester recommendations and structural funds. In an interview, a German official deplored the fact that this provision had so far been a "toothless tiger." However, Berlin has not given up on the idea of using EU spending as a leverage tool. In September 2015, Schäuble proposed that "national projects which benefit from financing from the European funds should be systematically designed to implement the country-specific recommendations. The commission needs to make this the precondition for financing national projects."[3]
– Flexibility: The German and Dutch governments support the idea of maximum flexibility within the EU budget as a way to react quickly to unforeseen events.
– Environmental and climate spending: In general, there is wide acceptance in Germany and the Netherlands that sustainability criteria and climate conditionality should be attached to EU spending. CAP direct payments are seen as too 'passive'. If the CDU and Greens formed a governing coalition after the 2017 elections, it would try to shift the boundaries towards a greener and more investment-orientated CAP. However, German officials warn that a bilateral agreement with France will be needed on the future of CAP. Traditionally, accommodating French preferences on the CAP has been a way for Germany to secure support for its own objectives. Also, the CSU – the Bavarian sister party of Angela Merkel's CDU – tends to defend agricultural subsidies.

France: between pro-EU and conservative instincts

The French position during the post-2020 MFF negotiations will be uncomfortable since its different objectives will be incompatible. Brexit and dire public finances will force France to adopt a conservative attitude toward the overall level of spending. This will make keeping the maintaining current spending on farmers' subsidies while raising eurozone, climate and Schengen spending very challenging. For other key players like the European commission and Germany, this expected lack of clarity and prioritisation will be difficult to deal with.

– Deflate the EU budget, create a eurozone budget: Whoever wins the French presidency next May, the government will be constrained by the need for prolonged fiscal consolidation. The French position on the MFF is likely to change marginally if a centre-right government takes office, since Les Républicains endorse, at least rhetorically, the northern European vision of a slimmer EU focused on key priorities. A new centre-left administration would, by contrast, seek to obtain higher EU spending for growth and social cohesion to offset fiscal belt-tightening at home.
– Own resources: Ensuring the EU has direct access to a solid pool of resources is a priority for the current French government. Finding a way to bypass the EU budget's tight boundaries and narrow focus on national contributions is something which appeals across the political spectrum. In an interview, a senior French official said this would be difficult, though not impossible if a flexible "basket of taxes" was available from which member states could pick and choose.
– Eurozone treasury and 'investment budget': Both the centre left and the centre right support the idea of a eurozone fiscal capacity, though its objectives, boundaries and financing are unclear. Hollande has made the case for a common investment capacity outside the EU budget. Les Républicains advocate a "European monetary fund" backed by a "European treasury."[4]

- Security: Future French governments are likely to support higher EU spending on police and justice cooperation, migration and border controls. Nicolas Sarkozy's flagship EU proposal is "Schengen 2," ie an inner circle within the Schengen area based on greater regulatory harmonisation and effective border controls. Frontex would also be reinforced.
- Agriculture: There is a consensus across the French political spectrum that the CAP budget should not diminish after 2020. Nonetheless, there is openness to further CAP reform towards greater redistribution, greening and market risks insurance (see section 3).
- A post-COP 21 EU budget: There is sympathy for the idea of matching the Paris climate agreement's ambitions with greater EU resources dedicated to environmental objectives. Paris could back more 'climate mainstreaming' across the EU budget, although it would resist this turning into more intrusive controls from the EU and it will not be a priority.

Poland (and the Visegrad group): on the defensive

The 'friends of cohesion' coalition is expected to remain in place, though more for ideological than rational reasons. Countries like the Czech Republic and Slovakia may become net contributors soon and have an interest in curtailing cohesion spending for less developed regions. However, the Visegrad group has higher priorities, such as avoiding greater burden sharing in the eurozone (including pre-in countries) and Schengen area.

- Overall spending and rules: Poland is comfortable with a tight budget and with extending German-inspired rules such as 'ex-ante' conditionality and performance-budgeting. These are seen as ways to keep (perceived) spendthrift governments in check, especially Mediterranean countries.
- Limiting an investment-based budget: Polish officials warn against the temptation to transform cohesion funds into an investment tool. They observe that cohesion funds are crucial public investment

drivers (EU co-financed public investment amounts to 50 per cent of the total in Poland). A strong view in Warsaw is that the commission should not "become a banker." Extending the EFSI model would only disadvantage catch-up regions and countries.

- Reluctance to expand headings three and four spending: For Poland, internal security and external affairs are national competences. On this question, a similar anti-migrant attitude has strengthened rather than loosened ties between central European governments on the left and right. At the very least, Warsaw would expect any rise in EU spending for security and external affairs to specifically help promote stability in the eastern neighbourhood (ie targeted towards helping manage tensions between Ukraine and Russia, rather than in the Middle East or Africa).

- Scepticism towards EU environmental spending: Poland reluctantly endorsed 'climate mainstreaming'. The current Law and Justice government is unlikely to welcome any further moves in that direction. Poland also considers farmers' recent difficulties as evidence that it will be difficult to depart from income support. 1.4m farms receive direct payments in Poland. The current conservative administration was instrumental in opposition in pushing the previous centre-right government to shift 25 per cent of the budget allocated to rural development (pillar one) to direct farmers' subsidies (pillar two). This position is unlikely to change in the next few years.

3. OPTIONS AND THE POLITICAL SPACE FOR CAP REFORMS

Why a new CAP reform is needed and how to initiate it

The relevance of the CAP and its significance in the EU budget has long been questioned. Since the 1980s, successive reforms have addressed some of the most negative effects of CAP, such as overproduction and poor environmental outcomes (see chapter 1). However, frustration with a policy which monopolises nearly 40 per cent of the EU budget without any strong evidence of European added value is widely shared across Europe. Thirty-one per cent of Europeans do not think the CAP is "fulfilling its role in protecting the environment and tackling climate change" – a figure which is particularly high not only in northern European countries but also in France (47 per cent).[5]

As Karl Falkenberg (2016), the former director-general for the environment and senior adviser to the European commission president wrote recently:

> "European agricultural policy has increased productivity tremendously and made the European Union not only largely self-sufficient, but even a large exporter of food products to the world. This achievement has come with a price: continued reduction of the number of farms and farm employment, larger specialised production units, leading to monocultures with considerable environmental impacts and food quality that is increasingly questioned by consumers. [...] Despite several reform projects of the CAP, its monetary benefits still largely go to large intensive farming practices. Long-term trends on rural employment, farming incomes and major environmental indicators for soil quality and biodiversity remain problematic."

There is comprehensive evidence of a decline in biodiversity in Europe, with most of it happening in farmland (which covers 45 per cent of the EU's territorial area). Figure 5.2 shows that the population of farmland bird species has been decreasing more dramatically since 1990 than the average of all common bird species. Common bird species (there are 167) include farmland species, the forest species and a further 94 common species. Various EU initiatives to halt the trend (agri-environment schemes under CAP pillar two, special protection areas under the birds directive, Natura 2000, and the EU Biodiversity strategy to 2020) have not been able to outweigh the negative effects of agricultural intensification, although there is some evidence that agri-environment measures have had an overall positive impact on biodiversity (Gamero et al, 2016).

For these reasons, and in the context of the implementation of the Paris climate agreement and the UN sustainable development goals

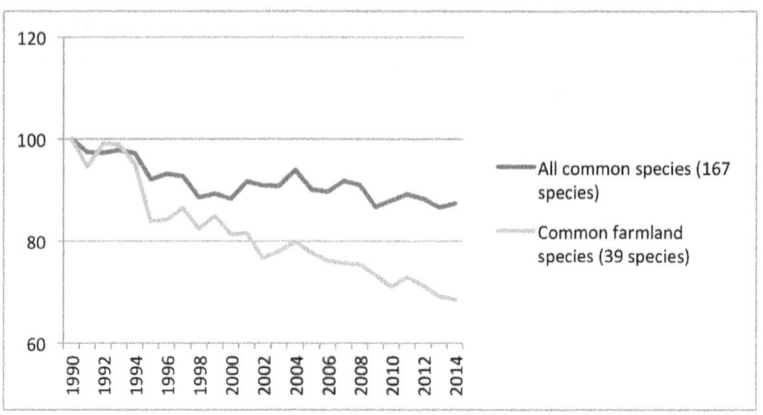

Figure 5.2 Common bird index (1990–2014), European Union (aggregate changing according to the context), Index (1990 = 100).* *Source*: Eurostat.

(both adopted in 2015), the CAP and its budget is likely to come under attack again during the next MFF negotiations. However, CAP reform advocates traditionally split into two categories: some want the share of agricultural spending substantially cut, while others call for a greener CAP with current spending levels maintained. The two objectives of a less spendthrift and greener CAP are not mutually exclusive, but they generate some tensions. In 2011–2013, a coalition of environmentalists and farmers successfully fought to defend the CAP budget while reinforcing environmental requirements. Yet, the former were ultimately disappointed. The outcome of the CAP reform finalised after the MFF agreement included only modest greening provisions. Also, 'pillar flexibility' in both directions meant that while some countries were able to transfer funds from pillar one direct payments to pillar two environmental subsidies, as had previously been the case, others were now able to reduce agri-environment spending to increase direct payments.

The debate on the post-2020 CAP has already started. The Dutch presidency organised an informal agriculture council in May 2016, ahead of which the Netherlands and France submitted position papers (see below). The French agriculture minister, Stéphane le

Foll, organised a meeting of the EU-27 agriculture ministers in early September to discuss the implications of the UK's departure for the future of the CAP. At the same time, a number of environmental pressure groups, national governments and MEPs have demanded a CAP 'fitness check' to be conducted in the context of the REFIT (regulatory fitness and performance) programme.

REFIT aims to make EU law simpler and reduce unnecessary regulatory burdens. Initiatives include the revision, withdrawal or removal of laws, as well as the implementation of evaluations and 'fitness checks'. In June 2016 the idea of a CAP fitness check was discussed at a meeting of the REFIT platform, which is chaired by Timmermans and brings together government and stakeholders.[6] Sixteen MEPs from various political groups and countries also wrote a letter to Juncker and Timmermans in July to back this request.[7] Some governments are wary of opening the door to another comprehensive CAP reform and argue that REFIT should deal only with more specific proposals.

The sections below first examine the ways of achieving a more environmentally friendly CAP, and then go on to look at the broader question of how the CAP could be structured in the future.

The greening dilemma: regulation or expenditure?

There are arguably three (not mutually exclusive) ways to achieve a greener CAP: extend pillar one conditionality; transfer money from pillar one to pillar two; and raise climate and biodiversity 'mainstreaming' through the whole EU budget, including CAP.

Option 1: Attach more ambitious green rules to direct payments

The commission's first year assessment of greening paints a mixed picture.[8] It finds that 72 per cent of EU agricultural area falls under the remit of at least one green direct payment obligation, therefore signalling "the potential to have a considerable impact." Yet, focusing specifically on the 'ecological focus areas' (EFA) obligation, the commission finds that the implementation options available to member states have led a vast number of farmers to implement measures with low returns on biodiversity. This finding echoes the IEEP (Hart, 2015, p.viii), who observe that "farmers who are not exempt from greening will be able to meet the requirements with very few changes in established management." Environmental pressure groups are generally hostile to greening, which they regard as a mere PR exercise to protect the agricultural subsidies system.

Several options are available to reinforce greening (see in particular Hart et al, 2016, p.40–46). An initial approach would consist of general rule changes, such as reducing exemptions so as to include more arable areas into the green payments systems, as well as attaching limitations on the use of pesticides or fertilisers. A second option would be to strengthen existing criteria (for instance, extending ecological focus areas from five to seven per cent). Finally, member states could be asked to design more ambitious measures from an EU menu of options which could include achieving greater greenhouse gas (GHG) sequestration, higher air and water quality or an improved better biodiversity performance.

An extension of greening could be cautiously welcomed by policymakers in Germany and France provided this does not mean greater bureaucratic burdens and, as far as France is concerned, lower support to vulnerable farmers. European citizens seem to welcome this option: according to a recent Eurobarometer survey, 87 per cent of them support green payments, with little variation across the EU.[9] Also, the commission seems determined to defend and embed greening into pillar one. In an interview, a source close to the agriculture commissioner said: "There will never be as much money for public goods in a [separate] green fund [as in CAP pillar one]."

Extending greening without increasing bureaucratic complexity would benefit from a flexible approach and a shift away from the current, prescriptive top-down one. Regional or national authorities could be offered a menu of broad environmental targets but given the choice of priorities and of the means to achieve them. This decentralised approach to greening would fit local conditions better and could find broad support. Challenges would arise, however, in ensuring that the targets are ambitious enough and are actually delivered, as well as ensuring the repayment of subsidies if they are not. The design of measures to achieve the targets should also avoid competitive distortions and be consistent with WTO 'green box rules'.[10]

Option 2: reduce the level of direct payments (pillar one) and raise contractual environmental spending (pillar two)

The main alternative to pillar one greening is to shuffle more money into pillar two. During the MFF 2014–2020 negotiations, greening was the main reason why the CAP budget was not reduced more dramatically than it was and why environmentalists did not obtain a significant reduction in pillar one spending. On the one hand, new financial constraints – such as the need to spend more on headings three and four – might impose a further cut in the CAP budget. On the other hand, disappointment with greening, and the lack of an agreement on how to take it forward, could justify expanding contractual support for investment in, or delivery of, environmental and social public goods to the detriment of direct income support. Raising financial incentives could make rural developments subsidies more attractive and efficient than uniform mandatory obligations.

Some voices have recently called for limiting direct payments and spend more on sustainability. Falkenberg (2016) argued that in "planning the next agricultural reform, more attention should be placed on sustainability, and strengthening rural development support type instead of direct payments linked to acreage." The German environment ministry has adopted even more radical rhetoric by talking about a "nature protection offensive." This would consist of abolishing the distinction between pillar one and two, and mainly funding climate- and environment-related projects. However, this vision does not necessarily reflect the German government view.

Environmental pressure groups tend to support more explicit spending on environmental public goods. However, they point to the risk of a 'watered down' pillar two under the pressure of the agricultural lobby in compensation for lower pillar one direct payments. To avoid this, strict climate and biodiversity targets could be attached to spending. The governance structure of the CAP could also be changed in a way that would give environmental officials and NGOs a greater say. This would restore trust in a policy perceived today as being controlled by agricultural officials in the commission, the council and the agriculture committee in the European parliament.

Cutting pillar one could be achieved either by capping payments to individual farmers or reducing payments to all farmers across the board. The first option would provide the opportunity to make the CAP more redistributive. The 2013 reform introduced optional capping above €150,000 but few countries took advantage of this possibility. Countries like France, Germany and Spain did not opt in (though they introduced other redistributive measures, see chapter 3). During the MFF 2014–2020 negotiations, the Green-EFA group in the European parliament proposed to cap direct payments at €100,000 and to shift saved resources to pillar two or other environmental objectives. In 2013, the French MEP José Bové found that such a cap would have an impact on only 3.5 per cent of EU farmers (450,000 out of 13 million) but help save €4.8bn/year which could be used "to support family farms and small and medium-sized operations [as well as] to initiate or strengthen other EU policies, such as construction of the infrastructure necessary for the energy transition to a low-carbon economy."[11]

Nonetheless, the political space for limiting direct payments and shifting more money to pillar two is constrained. In 2011–2013, the commission failed to impose mandatory capping, mainly due to the opposition of Germany and the UK. Germany opposed it due to the presence of large farms in eastern Germany (a legacy of the Communist past), something which is not likely to change in the near future. French officials say they are not closed to the idea of capping direct payments, but they are unlikely to throw their weight behind

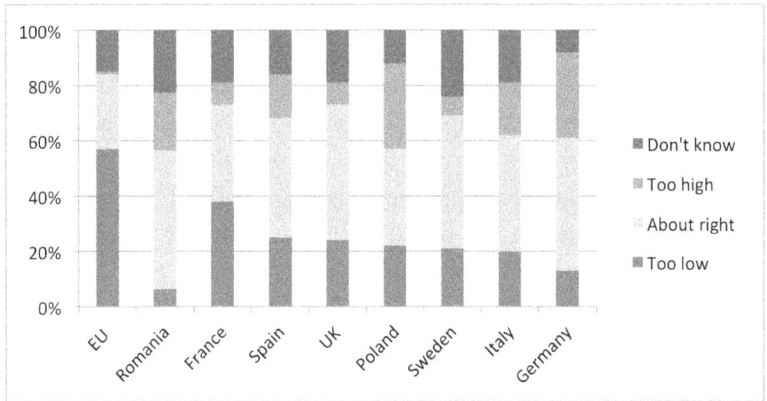

Figure 5.3 EU citizens' opinion on the level of financial support to farmers (2015). *Source*: Special Eurobarometer 440.

it. The fact that some environmental NGOs and food charities are among the largest direct payment recipients complicates the matter. Arguably, however, the removal of the UK – historically one of the firmest opponents of caps on payments – from the debate on the CAP's future could change the dynamic in this area.

Crucially, Europeans do not perceive large subsidies as a problem. Recent Eurobarometer data show that only a minority of them think the level of support for farmers is too high despite representing almost 40 per cent of the EU budget (see figure 5.2). The figures show little variation from 2005. When asked whether there should be an increase in EU financial support to farmers in the next 10 years, Nordic countries, Italy and Germany appear to be the most CAP-sceptic countries, while eastern European countries call for greater support.

Option 3: reinforce climate and biodiversity mainstreaming

A third option would be to expand climate and biodiversity 'mainstreaming' throughout the whole EU budget, harnessing new international constraints. As a consequence, climate and environmental spending would have to be raised within both CAP pillars (regardless of their volume).

In 2013, agriculture represented almost 10 per cent of the EU's total GHG emissions, a proportion that has not changed since 1990. Methane and nitrous oxide are the most prevalent gas emitted in agriculture. In volume, agriculture emissions dropped by 23 per cent between 1990 and 2013, a figure in line with the EU average performance (24 per cent). This achievement is better than the EU's objective of cutting GHG emissions by 20 per cent in 2020 from their 1990 levels. Yet, the European commission's projections suggest agriculture emissions will remain stable between 2013 and 2020 (see table 5.3), something which appears to undermine the need to continue on this trajectory.[12] Indeed, the EU's commitment – ahead of the Paris international conference on climate change in December 2015 – to cut emissions by 40 per cent in 2030 has set the bar very high.

In order to achieve its overall emissions target, the EU relies on three main types of instruments: the emissions trading scheme (ETS) covering the power and industry sector; binding national targets under the 'effort sharing' decision (covering the non-ETS sectors), the renewable energy directive and the energy efficiency directive; and the EU budget, though 'climate mainstreaming'. Climate mainstreaming consists of the commitment to spend 20 per cent of the EU budget 2014–2020 on climate-related actions. Raising this figure could have a significant impact on the design and delivery of EU spending programmes, although classifying expenditure as climate-relevant risks encountering technical difficulties and becoming a hostage to political considerations.

Table 5.4 Greenhouse gas emissions by the agricultural sector in the EU (1990–2013)

	Share in 1990 total emissions	Share in 2013 total emissions	Change 1990–2013 (volume)	Change 2013–2020 (projections)
EU	10%	9.8%	-22.6%	0%

Source: European commission.

Thirty per cent of the CAP budget is, in theory, related to climate action today. This includes 30 per cent pillar one green payments and 30 per cent climate-related expenditure within pillar two. The EU has also been mainstreaming biodiversity objectives throughout the EU budget, though it has not set a numerical target and mainly relies on non-binding methodological guidance. 'Biodiversity proofing' builds upon the 2011 EU biodiversity strategy to 2020, itself strongly related to the birds and habitats directives.

Going beyond the status quo would mean setting a 40 or 50 per cent climate and biodiversity objective and developing a more thorough way of defining and tracking relevant expenditure. Within pillar one, in order to address the current criticism, a higher share of green payments could be justified by the introduction of new criteria and/or national plans (see measures suggested in option 1). Within pillar two, only two of the six EAFRD objectives are related to biodiversity and climate change today. Member states could be forced to spend 50 per cent of their rural developments envelope on these objectives.

Options for restructuring the CAP

The contours of the future CAP is not only down to the future of greening, but also raises questions as to the overall level of expenditure, the type of income support in the face of higher price volatility and the type of investments which are necessary for European farmers to remain competitive. Some leaders and stakeholders have already suggested some ideas about restructuring in this context. Three contributions are particularly worth noting.

An integrated, tier-system (IEEP contribution)

In a report published in April 2016, the IEEP sets out four "future options for greening." The fourth (and most radical) option suggests redesigning the CAP as a "a single integrated set of measures structured in a tiered hierarchy" (Hart et al, 2016, p.49–50). The

CAP would not be based on two pillars anymore, but on four tiers of payments:

1. Basic payment, as compensation for high environmental and animal welfare standards, to provide insurance against climate and environmental risks, or for the maintenance of extensive and diverse and farm systems.
2. Payments for areas facing natural constraints.
3. Payment for higher environmental achievements.
4. Payments for specific environmental outcomes.

This option faces substantial administrative and political challenges, but it could gain traction if the current commission's efforts to simplify do not bear significant fruits. However, as the authors observe, the future CAP will need to find the right balance between general support and targeted incentives and between environmental outcomes and food production. The diversity of EU agriculture and climate change call for a flexible, tailor-made approach combining a "common EU structure" with "regional targeting" (Hart et al, 2016, p.58).

An investment-orientated CAP (Dutch contribution)

The Dutch contribution puts forward the vision of a new, integrated "agriculture and food policy," with three ambitious goals: more investment in digital technology and innovation; a greater contribution to climate transition (extension of greening); and an unambiguous market orientation while offering farmers a safety net based on price volatility rather than direct income support.[13]

More resources to face crises (French contribution)

In France, the combination of lower direct payments and the end of quotas is seen as having had a negative impact on small, vulnerable farms. The French contribution to the Dutch presidency informal agriculture council shares most of the assumptions of the Dutch contribution, but differs on the means to achieve these goals.[14] Coupled direct payments – payments based on the level of production – would still have a role to play within pillar one in order to set targeted production incentives. Support to innovation and investment measures could have a greater role to play within pillar two, however this also means targeting social innovation and agri-environment-climate measures. Greening would both be simplified and extended to a fourth requirement, "retaining crop coverage over the year." Finally, an income stabilisation tool would be put in place to compensate farmers for losses exceeding 30 per cent of their turnover. It would be financed by "mandatory precautionary savings" and would replace the existing crisis reserve.

Conclusion

There is scope for further and, perhaps, more meaningful restructuring of the CAP after 2020. The need to shift more EU resources towards priorities such as security and external affairs will put the CAP budget under pressure. Moreover, the EU's recent sustainability commitments justify reviewing the whole EU budget in the light of environmental and climate objectives. This double constraint justifies either reducing direct payments (while partially raising pillar two subsidies in compensation) or substantially beefing-up their climate and environmental conditionality. This could only be accepted if member states are given more flexibility both to subsidise their own farmers when they are faced with price volatility (for instance via higher state aid ceilings, something which nonetheless bears significant risks of distortion) and through the introduction of a new balance between EU objective- and target-setting on the one hand, and national discretion at the implementation stage on the other. Such comprehensive reform packages would certainly not please all EU capitals, but they have the potential to garner enough political support to get through.

NOTES

1. "Speech by Vice-President Kristalina Georgieva at the EU Presidency Conference on the Multiannual Financial Framework." January 28, 2016. Accessed August 2016, https://ec.europa.eu/commission/2014–2019/georgieva/announcements/speech-vice-president-kristalina-georgieva-eu-presidency-conference-multiannual-financial-framework_en
2. "EU Budget focused on results: Keynote speech by Wolfgang Schäuble." September 22, 2015. Accessed August 2016, http://www.bundesfinanzministerium.de/Content/EN/Reden/2015/2015-09-28-keynote-eu-budget-focused-on-results.html
3. *ibid.*
4. "Le projet des Républicains pour 2017." http://www.republicains.fr/projet, 247
5. "Special Eurobaromter 440. Report. Europeans, agriculture and the CAP." January 2016 (field work: October 2015). http://ec.europa.eu/COMMFrontOffice/PublicOpinion/index.cfm/ResultDoc/download/DocumentKy/69756, 27, 31
6. In March 2016, 115 NGOs coordinated by the EEB sent a letter to Juncker "to initiate an in-depth review of food production and consumption in Europe by conducting a Fitness Check of the Common Agricultural Policy (CAP)." See "115 NGOs call for major review of EU food and farming policy," European environmental bureau, March 22, 2016. Accessed August 2016 http://www.eeb.org/index.cfm/news-events/news/ngos-call-for-major-review-of-eu-food-and-farming-policy/ . The demand was examined at the "Second meeting of the REFIT Platform," June 26, 2016, http://ec.europa.eu/smart-regulation/refit/refit-platform/docs/28062016_platform_agenda.pdf , point 18: "Agriculture "Effectiveness and Efficiency of the CAP"
7. "Cross-compliances," the EAFRD , the "overlap between pillar one and pillar two" and "marketing standards for fresh fruit and vegetables" were the other items on the agenda at the 28 June 2016 meeting.
8. "Review of greening after one year." European commission communication, June 22, 2016, SWD(2016) 218 final, Part 1/6. Accessed August 2016, http://ec.europa.eu/agriculture/direct-support/pdf/2016-staff-working-document-greening_en.pdf
9. "Special Eurobaromter 440. Europeans, agriculture and the CAP. Summary." January 2016 (field work: October 2015). http://ec.europa.eu/COMMFrontOffice/PublicOpinion/index.cfm/Survey/getSurveyDetail/instruments/SPECIAL/surveyKy/2087, 17 (English version)

10. Under WTO rules, domestic support to agriculture falls into two categories: support measures with no, or minimal, distortive effect on trade on the one hand (often referred to as 'Green Box' measures) and trade-distorting support on the other hand (often referred to as 'Amber Box' measures). See more on the WTO website, accessed August 2016, https://www.wto.org/english/tratop_e/agric_e/ag_intro03_domestic_e.htm

11. "Time has come for a fairer CAP. A document by José Bové." The Greens-EFA in the European parliament. March 01, 2013. Accessed August 2016, http://eat-better.greens-efa.eu/time-has-come-for-a-fairer-cap-9412.html

12. "Climate action progress report 2015." European commission. November 18, 2015. COM(2015) 576 final. Accessed August 2016, http://ec.europa.eu/clima/policies/strategies/progress/docs/progress_report_2015_en.pdf, 23-24

13. "Food for the future. The future of food. Discussion paper of the Netherlands presidency." May 24, 2016. Accessed August 2016, https://english.eu2016.nl/documents/publications/2016/05/31/food-of-the-future

14. "A reformed CAP for competitive, sustainable and resilient agriculture." May 31, 2016. Accessed August 2016, http://agriculture.gouv.fr/amsterdam-stephane-le-foll-presente-une-vision-et-des-propositions-concretes-pour-une-pac-post-2020

CONCLUSION AND RECOMMENDATIONS

Debates on the EU budget naturally tend to focus on rough figures and net balances and one can expect the MFF mid-term review and next MFF negotiations to be no exception. Making up for the UK's net contribution after Brexit will certainly occasion a few sleepless night in Brussels. Beyond this, achieving a better and more meaningful EU budget is not simply a matter of the level of spending. At a time when fiscal resources are constrained, and when EU member states face new migration and security pressures while having committed themselves to very ambitious sustainability targets, the question of the quality of EU spending should receive much more attention. So, too, should the interrelated questions of what justifies EU intervention and in which areas, and how the EU can best use spending to advance specific goals.

This publication started from the assumption that the level of resources at the disposal of the EU will stay broadly the same in the next five to 10 years. The ongoing debate on 'own resources' is unlikely to bear significant fruits in the current political climate. Yet even at its current size, the EU budget has far-reaching implications on national and regional spending. Embedding expenditure into recognised public goods and goals, and setting the right rules and targets for EU spending programmes, should be a matter of concern far beyond the 'Brussels beltway'.

The historical overview provided here has stressed the continuing weight of the legacy of past decisions and commitments and analysed the latest attempts to reform the EU budget, especially during the last MFF negotiations. Efforts by the European commission, the parliament and some member states to 'rationalise' the budget have produced a useful debate on 'European added value', and interesting innovations such as: ex-ante, macroeconomic and environmental conditionalities; performance-based budgeting; climate mainstreaming; and financial instruments. The share of investment-orientated spending has increased vis-à-vis 'passive' cohesion and agricultural subsidies. However, the scope for improvement remains huge.

The 2016–2017 MFF mid-term review may not be the time for a major restructuring of the EU budget, but it provides the opportunity for a stocktaking exercise in preparation for the next MFF. Moreover, Brexit will necessarily shake the current equilibrium and compel net contributors to assess more thoroughly the relevance of EU spending. **A double ambition should guide the discussions leading up to the adoption of the post-2020 MFF: focusing the EU budget more clearly on supporting sustainable economic and social models and creating a more flexible budget to react to new circumstances and adapt to local needs and preferences.** On the basis of the interviews conducted for this research, such a reform agenda would have considerable traction since it would directly address public and governmental concerns.

The following recommendations provide more specific suggestions on how such a vision could be implemented.

RECOMMENDATIONS FOR A MEANINGFUL MID-TERM REVIEW

- Mobilise sufficient resources to compensate EFSI-related cuts affecting Horizon 2020 and the connecting Europe facility,

maintain the youth employment initiative, and cover increased requirements and new initiatives on migration and external action.
- To do so, revise downwards allocations for under-used programmes, mobilise available margins under ceilings, carry over surpluses and double the size of the €1bn per year flexibility instrument.
- Establish greater consistency between different investment-orientated instruments (ESI funds, EFSI and other financial instruments).
- As part of the 'EU budget focused on results' initiative, develop performance benchmarks linked to the Europe 2020 targets to be applied to all headings one and two programmes. Clarify the commission's definition of climate mainstreaming and the current method for tracking climate action.
- On the occasion of sectoral policy reviews (to be conducted in the first half of 2017), or as part of the REFIT platform, run a CAP 'fitness check' with the view to preparing further CAP reform (similar to the CAP health check carried out in 2008, but with higher ambitions).

RECOMMENDATION FOR A QUALITY POST-2020 EU BUDGET

- Make a virtue of necessity. Assume the EU budget will stay at one per cent of GNI (with possible embryonic eurozone fiscal capacity). Focus on improving budget quality and flexibility.
- As a first step into the post-2020 MFF discussions, develop a European added value definition and framework. The could entail identifying what EU public goods are and why spending at EU level or coordination by the EU of national spending has a better chance of achieve them than (uncoordinated) national spending. This debate should be linked to the elaboration of the EU's post-2020 sustainability strategy. The opportunity for a large public consultation or deliberative process should not be missed.

- Shift more money towards areas of clear EAV, such as research and innovation, trans-EU infrastructure, migration and security, external action and environmental protection. Savings could come from repatriating regional policy for rich regions (or limiting it to financial instruments) and capping agriculture direct payments at €100,000 per holding, two measures which, if combined, could potentially save up to €100bn over seven years.[1] Resistance to a cut in EU funding in specific areas (eg cohesion policy and direct payments) could be eased by relaxing state aid rules.
- By default, extend 'ex-ante' (governance), macroeconomic and environmental conditionalities. Reinforce enforcement mechanism and incentives, for instance, by extending performance-based payments. Provide more support for administrative capacity to drive structural change.
- Enhance flexibility within and outside the EU budget and at the implementation stage. Unused envelopes, margins and surpluses should be easier to mobilise. Alternatively, the ratio of special (flexibility) instruments could be raised up to five per cent of the MFF volume, instead of its approximately one per cent level today. The way in which EU money is spent at national and regional level could be subject to greater discretion, provided authorities set out plans to achieve specific objectives and targets reflecting EU public goods.

Specific recommendations: Towards a greener CAP and EU budget

- Path dependency scenario: Modest environmental outcomes
    - Reduce pillar one direct payments but leave some flexibility for national support for farmers, especially in cases of price volatility. National support would be subject to environmental conditions.
    - Extend environmental conditionality within pillar one, for instance by pushing the green payments share up to 40 or 50 per cent, and improve the effectiveness of existing rules and eligibility criteria.

CONCLUSION AND RECOMMENDATIONS 103

- End flexibility from pillar two to pillar one and require member states to increase support to pillar two agri-environment-climate measures as a consequence of the transfer.
- Ambitious scenario: Significant environmental outcomes
  - Reorganise CAP to reflect clear European added value: investment towards higher standards, income stabilisation and nature management.
  - Consolidate environmental conditionality within the investment and income stabilisation functions by assigning regional or national authorities headline environment-climate targets such as lower greenhouse gas emissions, biodiversity and water quality.
  - Substantially raise resources towards rural development and nature protection and restoration through the EAFRD and LIFE+ programmes.
- Radical shake-up scenario 3: Highest sustainability outcomes
  - Make the future EU budget the main instrument to achieving more sustainable development socio-economic models in the EU by linking it directly to the EU's post-2020 sustainability strategy.
  - Substantially raise climate and biodiversity 'mainstreaming' throughout the EU budget (for instance up to 50 per cent) based on a more robust definition of relevant expenditure and strong governance.
  - Transform CAP into a 'rural development, nature and food policy': remove direct income support linked to acreage and strictly subsidise investment and activities linked to employment, nature protection and restoration, and sustainable production in rural areas.

NOTE

1. Funding for more developed regions: €54bn (2014–2020). Direct payments of more than €100,000 represented 17 per cent of the EU-28 total direct payments in 2015 (see "Report on the distribution of direct aids to

agricultural producers (financial year 2014)." http://ec.europa.eu/agriculture/cap-funding/beneficiaries/direct-aid/pdf/annex2-2014_en.pdf , 6). The 2014–2020 total figure for direct payments and market measures is €278bn. Seventeen per cent of €278bn = €47bn. €54bn + €47bn = €101bn.

REFERENCES

Alesina, Alberto, Ignazio Angeloni, and Ludger Shuknecht. "What Does the European Union Do?." *Public Choice* 123 (2005): 275–319.

Giovanni Anania and Maria Rosaria Pupo D'Andrea. "The 2013 Reform of the Common Agricultural Policy." in *The Political Economy of the 2014–2020 Common Agricultural Policy An Imperfect Storm* edited by John Swinnen, 33–86, Brussels: Centre for European Policy Studies (CEPS), London: Rowman and Littlefield International, 2015.

European Union Budget Reform: Institutions, Policy and Economic Crisis, edited by Giacomo Benedetto and Simona Milio, Basingstoke: Palgrave Macmillan, 2013.

Bertelsmann Stiftung. "The European Added Value of EU Spending: Can the EU Help its Member States to Save Money? Exploratory Study." Gütersloh: Bertelsmann Stiftung, 2013.

Gabrielle Ciprianni. *Financing the EU budget. Moving forward or backwards?*, Brussels: Centre for European Policy Studies (CEPS), London: Rowman and Littlefield International, 2014.

Ecorys, Nederland BV, Netherlands Bureau for Economic Policy Analysis (CPB) and Institute for Economic Research (IFO). "A study on EU spending. Final report." June 24, 2008. Accessed August 2016. http://agriregionieuropa.univpm.it/sites/are.econ.univpm.it/files/FinestraPAC/Editoriale_12/study_EUspending_en.pdf

Karl Falkenberg. "Sustainability Now! A European Vision for Sustainability." European commission, EPSC Strategic Notes Issue 18/2016. Last modified July 20, 2016. http://ec.europa.eu/epsc/publications/notes/sn18_en.htm

Anna Gamero, Lluís Brotons, Ariel Brunner, Ruud Foppen, Lorenzo Fornasari, Richard D. Gregory, Sergi Herrando, David Hořák, Frédéric Jiguet, Primož Kmecl, Aleksi Lehikoinen, Åke Lindström, Jean-Yves Paquet, Jiří Reif, Päivi M. Sirkiä, Jana Škorpilová, Arco van Strien, Tibor Szép, Tomáš Telenský, Norbert Teufelbauer, Sven Trautmann, Chris A.M. van Turnhout, Zdeněk Vermouzek, Thomas Vikstrøm, Petr Voříšek. "Tracking progress towards EU biodiversity strategy targets: EU policy effects in preserving its common farmland birds." *Conservation Letters*, http://onlinelibrary.wiley.com/doi/10.1111/conl.12292/epdf preserving its common farmland birds

Kaley Hart. "Green direct payments: implementation choices of nine Member States and their environmental implications." Institute for European Environmental Policy (IEEP). September 2015. http://www.ieep.eu/assets/1890/IEEP_2015_Green_direct_payments_-_implementation_choices_of_nine_Member_States_and_their_environmental_implications.pdf

Kaley Hart, David Baldock and Allan Buckwell. "Learning the lessons of the Greening of the CAP." Institute for European Environmental Policy (IEEP). April 2016. http://cap2020.ieep.eu/assets/2016/4/20/Learning_the_lessons_from_CAP_greening_-_April_2016_-_final.pdf

Alexandra Huza. "The cohesion versus better spending debate during the negotiation of the EU MFF 2014–2020," *Knowledge Horizons - Economics* 6,2 (2014): 91–99. Accessed August 2016 http://www.orizonturi.ucdc.ro/arhiva/2014_khe_6_pdf/khe_vol_6_iss_2_91to99.pdf

Alan Mathews. "The Multi-Annual Financial Framework and the 2013 CAP Reform." in *The Political Economy of the 2014–2020 Common Agricultural Policy An Imperfect Storm* edited by John Swinnen, 169–214, Brussels: Centre for European Policy Studies (CEPS), London: Rowman and Littlefield International, 2015.

Arnout Mijs and Adriaan Schout. "Flexibility in the EU Budget. Are There Limits?" Clingendael report, December 2015. Accessed August 2016, http://www.clingendael.nl/sites/default/files/Flexibility%20in%20the%20EU%20Budget%20december%202015.pdf

Richard A Musgrave. *The theory of public finance; a study in public economy*. New York: McGraw-Hill, 1959.

Eulalia Rubio, David Rinaldi, Thomas Pellerin-Carlin. "Investment in Europe: Making the best of the Juncker Plan." Notre-Europe Jacques-Delors Institute, March 2016. Accessed August 2016, http://www.institutdelors.eu/media/investmentjunckerplan-rubiorinaldipellerincarlin-jdi-mar16.pdf?pdf=ok

LIST OF ABBREVIATIONS

ALDE	Alliance of Liberals and Democrats for Europe
AMIF	Asylum, migration and integration fund
ANC	Areas of natural constraints
CAP	Common agricultural policy
CDU	Christian Democratic Union (Germany)
COP21	UN framework on climate change Conference of Parties, 2015 Paris climate conference
CSU	Christian Social Union (Bavaria)
CEF	Connecting Europe facility
COSME	Programme for competitiveness of enterprises and SMEs
DCI	Development cooperation instrument
EAFRD	European agricultural fund for rural development
EAV	European added value
ECR	European Conservatives and Reformists
EEB	European environmental bureau
EEC	European Economic Community
EFA	Ecological Focus Area
EFSI	European fund for strategic investments
EGAF	European globalisation adjustment fund
EIB	European Investment Bank
EMFF	European maritime and fisheries fund

LIST OF ABBREVIATIONS

EMU	European monetary union
ENI	European neighbourhood instrument
EPP	European People's party
ERDF	European regional development fund
ESI (funds)	European structural and investment funds (include ERFD, CF, ESF, EARDF and EMFF)
ETS	Emissions trading scheme
FBS	Friends of better spending
FC	Friends of cohesion
FEAD	Fund for European aid to the most deprived
GAC	General affairs council
GDP	Gross domestic product
GHG (emissions)	Greenhouse gas emissions
GNI	Gross national nncome
Green-EFA	The Greens – European Free Alliance
IEEP	Institute for European Environmental Policy
IPA	Instrument for pre-accession
ISF	Internal security fund
LIFE+	EU's funding instrument for the environment and climate action
MEP	Member of the European parliament
MFF	Multiannual Financial Framework
NGO	Non-governmental organisation
R&D	Research and development
REFIT	Regulatory fitness and performance programme
S&D	Progressive Alliance of Socialists and Democrats
SURE	Special (European parliament) committee on policy challenges and budgetary resources for a sustainable European Union after 2013
TFEU	Treaty on the Functioning of the European Union
TOR	Traditional own resources
VAT	Value added tax
WTO	World Trade Organisation
YEI	Youth employment initiative

www.ingramcontent.com/pod-product-compliance
Ingram Content Group UK Ltd.
Pitfield, Milton Keynes, MK11 3LW, UK
UKHW020820240326
469204UK00019B/129